YOU ARE WORTHY

Stop Building Other People's Dreams and Sabotaging Your Own So You Can Step into Your Calling and Live Your Purpose with Confidence

KATHERINE NORLAND

YOU ARE WORTHY

Stop Building Other People's Dreams and Sabotaging Your Own So You Can Step into Your Calling and Live Your Purpose with Confidence

KATHERINE NORLAND

YOU ARE WORTHY

Stop Building Other People's Dreams and Sabotaging Your Own So You Can Step into Your Calling and Live Your Purpose with Confidence

Special FREE Bonus Gift for You

To help you achieve more success, there are **FREE BONUS RESOURCES** for you at:

FreeGiftFromCoachKat.com

You'll get three in-depth training videos from my online course "You Are Worthy" to show you that no matter where you've been or what you've done, you can become an heir to God's promises and live an empowering, noteworthy life with joy and accomplishment!

Katherine Norland

WHAT OTHERS ARE SAYING ABOUT KATHERINE NORLAND AND HER STRATEGIES

"Katherine's heart, encouragement and positivity are incredibly inspiring."

—Dhar Mann, Mission Driven Entrepreneur, CEO, and Founder of LiveGlam and Dhar Mann Studios

"I love how Katherine uses her own journey to show how she went through some tough obstacles in her life to become the woman she is today! Katherine's book has truly hit home…"

—Robert J. Moore, 5x International Bestseller, Guinness World Record Holder, Featured in Forbes

"Katherine Norland has done it. She has followed Jesus into the freedom He gives, and you can too!!! Read this book!!!"

—Pastor Rick Wright, The Gathering Place Church, Burbank, California

"…this book offers an incredible salvation roadmap that will save lives globally. Based on her own life experiences, Katherine offers thought-evolving explanations and concrete solutions towards building a critical spiritual foundation that we all need to bulletproof and empower our lives."

—Anyck Turgeon, Master Transformation Coach, Certified Grief Counsellor, Minister, and International Speaker

"Katherine has a unique and personal way of articulating a look at life, its challenges, and its successes. Without a doubt, I would highly recommend that you contact Katherine and hire her to become your next coach, or speaker."

—Is-Pi-Mik-Ki-Ew High Eagle, Joseph Henry Morsette, MSCJA, JD, LL.M.; International Consultant, prosecutor, public defender, judge, Indigenous combat veteran

"I've had a Skid Row & Prison Ministry for 39 years. I have counseled men & women for years in prisons... dark places where they could have changed their lives with Katherine's wonderful and insightful book. This is how powerful this book is because it covers all of what we go thru from youth to choices as an adult. I have purchased her books and given them to women that I counseled. EVERYONE was blessed and helped on their way to being healed."

—Mel Novak, Actor in over 70 movies (fought Bruce Lee in *Game of Death*)

"Katherine, thank you for telling your story with such authenticity and courage ... You are brave and you are an encouragement! This quote from your book is of many that captured my heart because it's such a fundamental principle for living a meaningful life and thriving in every area of life. 'God wants to work through you and do something amazing with you, and He will if you believe, trust Him, and ask Him for help.' Good book!"

—Kay Kgaogelo Olorunju, Founder, Personal and Professional Life Coach at Living Seeds, Norway

"If you are finding yourself in a place of putting other people's needs and dreams above yours, I'd recommend getting this book!"

—Danielle Pomerleau, Authenticity Coach to Christian Entrepreneurs, Tulsa, Oklahoma

"WOW... What a great read! I love the honesty, authenticity, and practical solutions that anyone from all levels of belief, spirituality and life can relate to and apply—to their daily lives!!"

—Monica Morton, Celebrity Private Detective/TV Pundit

"...life enriching, truth that needs to be told ... Beautiful story telling bringing the reader in and closer to God throughout ... A must read!"

—Kathy Graves Farley, Leadership Speaker, Author, CEO at Arrowhead Ranch Outdoor Science School & Conference Center, California

"Katherine is such an inspiring coach, and you will find implementing her teachings rewarding and transformational in themselves ... I would highly recommend Katherine to any client on their journey of self-discovery, inner healing or even re-discovery, especially following events and traumas that affected this area. This book is certainly material for rebuilding strength in the inner man and the needed self-confidence development and productivity, and/or increased success!"

—Iris C. Luke, Author, Faith-based Coach, and Counselling Therapist, Founder of TrophyPillars Int'l (London, United Kingdom)

"*You are Worthy* ... is rich with wisdom on the subject of self-worth developing, growing in confidence, and in remembering Whose we are, and who we are in Whom we have believed, and therefore should be getting our value from.... Katherine is clearly an expert on this subject, and her dynamic delivery style and proven success strategies are must-haves for an exciting personal improvement journey."

—Lishah Luke
Musician, Songwriter, and Content Creator

"As a fellow suicide survivor, I felt Katherine could relate to many serious struggles I've gone through and also those that women in general go through. I appreciated Katherine's light-hearted approach and truly appreciated and applaud Katherine for sharing vulnerably, candidly and transparently in order to get this highly important message across."

—Violet Detre, Happiness Advocate, Speaker,
Best-selling author of *Ready, Set, Go!* with Brian Tracy

Retail: 19.95

Special Quantity Discount

5-20 Books	**$17.95**
21-99 Books	**$15.95**
100-499 Books	**$13.95**
500-999 Books	**$11.95**
1000+ Books	**$9.95**

To place an order, contact:

Katherine@KatherineNorland.com

The Ideal Professional Speaker For Your Next Event!

Hire Katherine Norland for a keynote, seminar, workshop, or training!

For any church, organization, school, or group that wants to be taught:

- How to stop building other people's dreams and sabotaging your own
- How to step into your calling and live your purpose with confidence
- How to walk into any room like you belong and are just as valuable as anyone else
- How to get to the root of your worthiness issues so you can be healed and set free
- How not to let your flaws stop you but make the best of what you've got
- How to make peace with yourself so you can be effective for God
- How to finally know you're enough just the way you are
- How to stop comparing yourself to others

To CONTACT or BOOK Katherine Norland to SPEAK:
Katherine@KatherineNorland.com

THE IDEAL ENCOURAGEMENT COACH FOR YOU!

If you're ready to overcome challenges, have major breakthroughs, and achieve higher levels, then you will love having Katherine Norland as your encouragement coach!

TO CONTACT Katherine Norland
Katherine@KatherineNorland.com

Dedication

It is with respect, admiration, and sincere appreciation that I dedicate this book to my wonderful family. My dad and mom, Donald and Arlene; my husband Robert; my two children, Timothy and Elijah; and my brother Tim. Without you and the lessons you've taught me throughout my life, I wouldn't have the blessing of being where I am today. Thank you from the bottom of my heart.

I love you dearly!

Contents

Preface

I used to think I was worthless—that I'd only have value if I looked better, was younger, smarter, thinner in some places and thicker in others, or had more money. I felt like I didn't measure up in many ways. It seemed impossible for me to find joy. I didn't know how to love myself. I thought I was fat, ugly, even hideous. I didn't think anyone wanted to be my friend.

I'd get so upset by things that would happen or what people would say that I'd cry over it for weeks. I felt hopeless. I thought I would never get better. I was imprisoned by my negative thoughts, thinking others had it so much better than I did, wondering why God even made me.

Back then, I was so shy and unsure of myself, I couldn't even order a pizza over the phone. For years, I was filled with anxiety and fear of rejection and confrontation. One time, I had to send my mom to the dry cleaners for me because I was too afraid to point out that they missed several stains when cleaning my dress, and they needed to clean it again.

But now, I'm unfazed by most offenses and challenges. I'm able to stand in front of large crowds of people and be vulnerable, sharing personal things about myself, including my failures. I've been able to reach goals I thought were impossible, even though I didn't starve myself slim, Botox my brains out, or buy a Brazilian butt. I never obtained that coveted doctorate, master's degree, or even a technical college education. I didn't go around fixing all the things I thought were stopping me from my dreams. Yet, by applying the lessons I learned and share in this book, I was able to have the confidence I needed—even with bad acne, not knowing fifth-grade math, or what proper sentence structure was.

Even though at the time, I didn't believe I had what it took, and didn't measure up to what I thought was ideal to help me win in life, I learned the single most important thing to help myself get unstuck. And that was that none of the outward things mattered. What did matter was that God believed in me, and He was rooting for me. And if He is for me, then no one could be against me (Romans 8:31). I had to learn how to overcome my biggest enemy: *me.* I had to decide not to be at war with myself any longer.

Because of that transformation, I'm now able to run wholeheartedly after all my dreams of writing books, acting (in over 100 films), shooting regularly for Dhar Mann Studios, directing and producing movies, and motivational speaking. Let me tell you, there was a lot I had to learn and overcome to be able to go from self-loathing to self-loving. I'm glad you picked up this book, because I want to show you how I was able to get rid of my self-hate, replace it with love, and finally know my worth, so that you can do the same.

I'm going to share with you what I learned when I didn't even think there was a purpose for me on Earth—when I felt worthless and ashamed of who I was, and convinced God made a mistake when He made me. You might feel the same, but you won't after reading this book. If you're a little further along on your journey and don't identify with hating yourself like I did, and you only came to bolster your value, hang with me; you'll find plenty in this book to either solidify your worth, or help you take how you see yourself to the next level and give you a different perspective to catapult you where you desire to go.

If you take to heart what I've written and follow the steps outlined in this book, you'll be able not only to call a truce with the person staring back at you in the mirror, but also to actually love them. So, stick with me until the end; you'll gain some powerful tools and mindset shifts to tackle whatever comes your way and know *You Are Worthy*, and your dreams are worth fighting for.

Introduction

If you're like me, knowing your worth has been a struggle for you. People may have said to you, "What's your problem? Just get over yourself; there's nothing wrong with you. You're fine, don't be too hard on yourself." Yet, at the same time, you may have had other people tell you your whole life that you're wrong and you never do anything right. Perhaps the harshest critic telling you those things is you.

But here's something you're doing right: You picked up this book, which means you're ready to stop allowing your negative thoughts about yourself, or other people's opinions, to keep you from pursuing the powerful future God has for you. Or maybe you don't even know God has a powerful future for you; you're just trying to get through the week, to make peace with the person staring back at you in the mirror, who you don't love very much right now.

Maybe you even think the people who've put you down and said awful things about you are right. Picking up this book might be your last effort to break out of your shell and find something to like about yourself or figure out if your life has any meaning or purpose. I don't take that for granted. We are all in different places on our journey.

But by reading this book and showing up for yourself, you've already shown your courage, and you're ready to do whatever it takes to make your life what *you* want it to be. I want you to know that you're not in this alone. God sees you and loves you. You never need to waste another day feeling bad about yourself.

I want you to know there *is* hope. If I can do it, you can do it. You have everything it takes to become the person you've always wanted to be, no matter where you are right now or what obstacles are standing in your way. Whether it stems from negative thoughts you have about yourself, someone in your life who constantly points out your faults, or God's enemy and ours, the devil, who made it his purpose to tell you lies that make you feel unworthy and unlovable, feeling bad about yourself stops today.

Right now, you might know God loves and cares about you because He's a good God. But you have a hard time getting that message from your head down into your heart. Yet, that's the key. Once I knew my worth in my soul and spirit, only then could I act on it. Beyond merely believing God cared, I had to embrace another truth tied into my worthiness issues, and that was that God wasn't upset with me or ashamed of me. And He's not upset with or ashamed of you either. He's not just putting up with you. He doesn't think you're a waste of His time. He doesn't even love others, who seem to have it all together and are serving Him better, more than He loves you.

I want you to know God thinks You Are Worthy; He made you just the way you are for a purpose. Nothing and no one can stop you from the dreams you desperately desire, unless you allow it. There's nothing about you that makes your dreams impossible to achieve. Not only is it okay to have dreams and desires, but if you delight yourself in Him, He'll also give you the desires of your heart (Psalm 37:4). He wants to help you all the way. He cares about you, and that includes everything that has you concerned. He wants to see you joyful, at peace, and full of hope (Romans 15:13). He wants to supply your every need (Philippians 4:19). More than you or anyone else, God wants you to live your best, most blessed life.

My hope is that through following my journey, you'll be able to look in the mirror and not cringe. You'll be able to ask that person out, talk to that person you considered "unapproachable," or develop that idea for the product or company you weren't sure would work. You'll be able to ask for a raise at work, or stand up and give a presentation without feeling foolish. You'll have the courage and confidence to speak to your partner about the things you've been afraid to mention, without thinking you'll lose them. There are dozens of other things you'll be able to do, right where you're at, even if nothing outwardly changes about you, by having a total makeover on the inside. You will see yourself as worthy and operate that way. That will affect the way others see you as well.

How to Go Through the Book

In this book, I'll share what I've been through and the key points and lessons I've learned along the way. If you want to highlight or underline in the book, that's great, please do; that way you can go back and find the parts that affected you.

I'll use stories and scriptures to show you the simple steps I took that moved me from being a quiet, timid mouse who felt like she didn't have anything to offer or didn't deserve to have her voice heard, to being a courageous, self- and God-assured woman who's no longer intimidated, knows her worth, and can speak up about what's important to her. It will be easy for you to implement these tips.

As you read this book, think of me as your mentor, or a really good friend who's simply giving you some heart-to-heart advice.

This book isn't meant to be an exhaustive study; I have an online course, also called "You Are Worthy," that does a deeper dive with fun illustrations, music, sound effects, videos, skits, and extra lessons.

What I'll be sharing with you worked not only for me but also for my coaching clients to find the freedom to be who they're meant to be and overcome obstacles brought on by an improper view of themselves. It's time to drop what weighs you down and, like an air balloon, lift high into the future you've been dreaming about.

What You'll Get Out of the Book

Here's what will happen if you apply what you read in this book: You'll be able to change your perspective about yourself and your situation in a positive way. You'll discover that God loves you and made you the way you are for a purpose. You'll become confident in who you are and not feel the need to compare yourself to others. You'll know where your true beauty comes from, and you'll start to have good days, no matter what you look like. You'll develop your heart and soul to be strong and not cave in to the pressures of others, but stand firm in your convictions. You'll make the separation between who you really are and the body you live in. You'll start making the best of what you've got and not be desperate to change it. You'll use what you assumed would disqualify you to actually win at life. You'll learn to leave your past behind, and not drag painful memories or reminders of who or what you could have been into your now, because your future is yet to be determined.

After reading this book, you'll finally know once and for all that You Are Worthy. You don't have to please others, and you matter just as much as anyone else. You'll be able to live your life unashamed of who you are, how God made you, or what your talents and capabilities are. You'll stop building other people's dreams and sabotaging your own, so you can step into your calling and live your purpose with confidence. You'll have the courage to go after your dreams and make your mark in this life.

My hope for you is that after you work through this book, you can walk into any room, sure of who you are and who God made you to be, without apology. And no matter who else is in the room or how important they are, or how they've treated you in the past, you'll know without a doubt that *you are worthy,* you belong, and you deserve to be there too.

Chapter One

See Yourself the Way God Does

What would your life be like if you could see yourself the way God sees you? If you could look at yourself and feel nothing but the deepest love? How much grace would you extend to yourself when you mess up? Would you put yourself down all the time and constantly point out your flaws? How quickly would you forgive yourself? Would you continue to be displeased with yourself for not being perfect, and obsess about your failures?

Or would you be like a loving and compassionate parent, who, if your little 4-year-old comes to you crying because they accidentally spilled their milk and says, "Mommy, Daddy, I'm sorry…" you'd hug them right away and say, "It's okay, don't you worry about it, I love you." You'd hold their hand and go with them to help clean up their mess and forget about it.

Imagine being able to show that kind of love for yourself. When you make a mistake, could you embrace yourself and say, "It's okay, don't worry about it, I love you, let's just go clean up the mess and forget about it"?

In case you think God only sees all your faults, flaws, and ugly sins; or even if you don't really know how God sees you, but you think it must not be in a very good light, I want to share a secret with you. The secret is, in God's eyes, you are more breathtaking than the sunset. Did you know that? He thinks you are stunning, magnificent, His finest creation. And He's pleased with you.

I want to share with you where I came from and what I used to think about myself when I was too bogged down and heavy from chewing on and ingesting the wrong thoughts. Then I'll share the transformation and total makeover I had after I allowed the word of God to renew my thoughts by showing me how God saw me. It's my aim for you to see yourself the way God sees you. Don't worry. It will be very good.

I almost gave up before I started

I was in my early 20s when I felt the tug on my heart to become an actress. I was shy and nervous, but the pull to act was so strong I couldn't ignore it anymore. There was no place for acting in my small town of Saint Peter, Minnesota, but I found an acting class I could take in Minneapolis, which was about a 180-mile round trip for me. The class was in a massive, drafty room with high ceilings. I looked around at all my fellow students, feeling insecure, keeping my head down, wondering if I'd made a mistake, giving myself the opposite of a pep talk. "What are you doing here? You're not cut out for this. You'll never make it as an actress. You don't look like an actress should look. No one would want to see you act. You don't have what it takes. Everyone is going to see you act like a fool. You don't know what you're doing. You're going to leave here embarrassed, wishing you'd never come." I started to sink down into myself and feel the weight of the discouraging self-talk—my shoulders slumped over; my head hung low.

I listened to the teacher say that acting is like painting. In painting, there are three primary colors, and all other colors come from mixing the primary ones. Likewise, in acting, there are three buckets of emotions, and all other emotions come from mixing the primary ones. He said those three emotion buckets were joy, anger, and sadness.

I scoffed to myself: "bucket of joy"? It was more like a thimble. I tried to shake myself out of my disparaging thoughts by imagining the buckets of emotions like buckets of paint—red must be anger; of course sadness is blue, which means yellow is joy. I started to zone out for the rest of his speech and wonder why I'd bothered to come to this class. How could I really hope that an acting career was in my future?

I tuned back in as the teacher said, "There will be times where we'll be required to cry on cue as an actor. The script may call for it, like if we're in a scene where our child is dying. Now we're going to do an exercise where we explore the sadness bucket. I want each of you, one at a time, to come up and show us something from your sadness bucket.

"Without using words, come to the front of the class and emote sadness to us." The teacher continued. "What helps is if you think of something sad that's really happened to you, then you have something to draw from. So if you need to, remember when your dog died, or when you didn't get picked for the baseball team, or your friends didn't want to hang out with you anymore. Use the memories of that painful time to help you."

One by one, each student got up and did their thing. Some were better than others. Some had what seemed to be real tears. Some faked it. Yet even the ones who were unable to pull out the emotion required still amazed me because they had the courage to stand up there and present themselves to a group of strangers and show their vulnerability unashamed. Before the last person went forward, I scooted behind some other students, trying to make myself invisible, hoping he'd forget I was there. But when everyone else had gone, he called me to the front of the class.

I felt a surge of fear. My heart thumped as fast as an ADHD jackrabbit kicking a speed bag. My head felt a bit wobbly. I ambled to the front of the class. I didn't make eye contact with anyone. I just stood there. Uncomfortable. Petrified. The teacher tried to encourage me. He reminded me what the exercise was. I listened, staring at the scuffs on the hardwood floor. He said, "There's no pressure; you don't have to *do* anything. Just start thinking about what makes you sad. And see if we can pick up on it."

Suddenly, I got an image in my mind, and within moments, my face was contorting. My brow was furrowing. My eyes were scrunching. I was doing that ugly smile you do when you try to avoid letting the tears come out. Soon, they streamed down my face. I sobbed uncontrollably. I couldn't stop. This sadness emotion poured out from the largest bucket I had; it was more like a thousand-gallon tank than a bucket. It was far more powerful than my fear and insecurity, which would've told me to go sit down or leave this place. But at that point, I was sucked in deep by my own world. The rest of the class faded away. It was just me and my sadness. And I was drowning in it.

Finally, I cried out every tear in me. I was emotionally spent, too tired to care what others thought of me anymore. I lifted my head and looked around at the others. They were stunned. Silent. Some were in awe. Some were feeling awkward and uncomfortable. I exhaled and tried to calm my breathing back down. The teacher seemed flabbergasted. He questioned me. "How did you do that? What were you thinking about? Was there a fire? A tragic death? Were you at your grandma's funeral?" I shook my head no. The teacher insisted. "What was it then?" I hung my head to hide my face. I took a deep breath. and I said, "I was just picturing myself … looking in the mirror."

I heard some snickering from the class, from those who thought I was kidding. But when it was clear I wasn't, the tension got thick. I could see out of the corners of my eyes the students shift and whisper to each other. I peeked around as people stared at me. Some looked confused. I felt shame rise in my throat, trying to choke me.

I panicked. Why did I tell anyone that? I should've lied and said I was thinking of something tragic. How did I allow myself to be so vulnerable? Why did I let my secret out? Now everyone knew my happy, smiling face was fake. It was a mask that helped me cover up the truth, a mask I'd been wearing for years to convince anyone who asked how I was that "I'm fine, everything's great," even though I felt like I was dying inside.

The teacher soon dismissed what I admitted, I guess not thinking or maybe not ready to address the idea that there might be something deeper going on with me. He said, "Well, whatever you were thinking, it worked. Remember that, because you can pull up that image and use it whenever you're doing a role where you need to show extreme sorrow or mourning."

A couple of students lifted their brows and shrugged at the teacher's suggestion. Others looked surprised, and still, some acted like I had just deceived everyone, and that this couldn't have been my first acting class. I sat there numb for the rest of the class because I knew that self-loathing and not even being able to look in the mirror without pain was my reality. In my mind, I was hideous, disgusting, fat and ugly. I was amazed that other students didn't seem to notice, or maybe they were just trying to be nice to the new kid.

As I drove home and replayed the events of the class in my mind, I imagined how terrible people really thought I was. But my thoughts kept getting pulled away. To my right, out of the passenger window, was one of the most beautiful and breathtaking sunsets I'd ever seen. I was in awe of God's creation. I began to wonder: why would God, who created this magnificent sunset, think it was worthwhile to create me?

That's the question we'll answer in this book. You're going to find out why God believed it was worthwhile to create you.

Chapter Two

God Created You *on* Purpose *for* a Purpose

Whatever God gave you and however He made you, no one can belay you if God wants to display you.

Do you believe God's wisdom is infinite? That He created you for this specific moment in time, to do something important? That He made you just the way you are, with a specific reason and purpose in mind? Do you think God has a plan He wants you to accomplish that nobody else can accomplish but you? What if I told you there's nothing about you—how you look, your age, your capabilities, what you've done or been through—that can stop you or hold you back from the big, beautiful purpose God made you for, no matter what anyone else's opinion of you might be … would you believe me?

Well, it's true. There's nothing about you or the circumstances you may be in that can disqualify you. God wants to work through you and do something amazing with you, and He will if you believe Him, trust Him, and ask Him for help. He can and will intervene and guide you to your destiny. Do you have any idea why God felt the need to make you? Are you wondering what you could possibly contribute to His plans? Or how you could make a difference on Earth? Do you believe God made you *on purpose for a purpose?*

While you're thinking about that, I'll share with you a couple of examples of two different women who had no idea they were important to God or that God would use them in such a big way, because they didn't seem to have much going for them.

The first was an orphan. Not only that, she was also Jewish. At the time, the Jews had been forced out of their country and were living in exile in Persia, where people hated them. However, God made this young lady beautiful. Her uncle found out that the King was having a beauty contest, and whoever was chosen as the most beautiful woman in all the land would become Queen.

The young woman entered the beauty contest, but she couldn't even reveal to anyone that she was Jewish, or she'd be in jeopardy of being disqualified. You may know by now that I'm talking about Esther. Though she was an orphan and a hated Jew, God used her beauty and the dignity she displayed for a greater purpose.

She won the beauty contest and was given the highest rank a woman could have. She was made the Queen. God also gave her favor in the sight of the King. The King listened to her at a time when women weren't really listened to. Because of that, she was able to save her people from Haman's evil plans to annihilate all the Jews. If you want to know more about Esther, I encourage you to read the book of Esther found in the Old Testament of the Hebrew Bible.

You may be thinking, "Well, she may have been from a hated tribe of people and living in exile without parents, but at least she was beautiful. You have a lot more advantages in life if you look good." But hold that thought. My second example is about Leah, who became Jacob's wife.

Unlike Esther, Leah was no beauty queen. She was plain. Her name means "weary," and she had weak, or "delicate," eyes. Some commentators have said that meant they were soft blue, which in those days was thought to be a blemish. Others have said bleary-eyed, which meant they had moisture in them, making them red and not agreeable to look at.

As a matter of fact, just to show you how outwardly undesirable she was, her own father had to fool Jacob into marrying her. Leah was not his first choice; her younger sister Rachel was. Rachel was described as beautiful in shape and stature, as well as being well-favored.

On at least one occasion, Leah even had to buy her husband's affection. She did this by giving her sister Rachel a bunch of mandrakes in return for getting her own husband to sleep with her. Why would Rachel want these mandrakes and allow her husband Jacob, who liked her the best and slept with her most nights, to go spend the night with Leah in exchange for them? Mandrakes are a plant in the nightshade family. They flower, and around the time of the wheat harvest, they produce fruit the size of a small apple. Some believed mandrakes would enhance a woman's fertility.

You see, there are some problems beauty can't fix. Rachel, though beautiful, was not fertile, even being the younger sister. She was not bearing children for her husband. Back in those days, that was the most important thing a woman could do. Her duty was to serve her husband and bear sons to carry on the family line. When Rachel demanded Leah's son give her the mandrakes he found, Leah said, "Wasn't it enough that you stole my husband? Now will you steal my son's mandrakes, too?" (Genesis 30:15 NLT). Here's something in the scripture that I found fascinating: it says, "When the LORD saw that Leah was not loved, he enabled her to conceive, but Rachel remained childless" (Genesis 29:31 NIV).

When God saw Leah was not loved, He blessed her much more than her sister, who was loved. When you read this story, you see God allowed Leah to bear four sons, while at the time, Rachel still hadn't borne any. By the time these two sisters, who were married to the same man, were done bearing children, Rachel had only borne two sons (four, if you count the two she had her maidservant bear for her), but Leah had borne six sons and a daughter. If you count the two her maidservant bore for her, it would be eight sons and a daughter.

Not only was God there helping Leah to make up for the pain she felt being unloved by her husband, but what's more is that Leah, even without being gorgeous like Esther or her sister Rachel, is the one God used to give birth to Judah, from whose line Jesus Christ was born, ushering in salvation to the world through her family line, not Rachel's.

JACOB LINEAGE TO JESUS

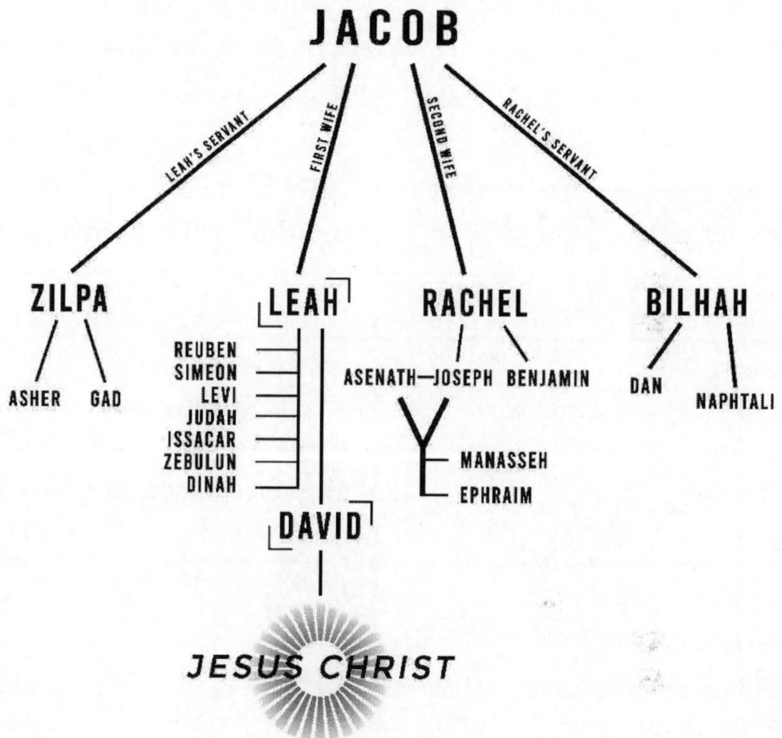

Let me just name a couple of men God used for great purposes, even though they had issues. Timothy, to whom two books of the Bible are written, was used mightily to spread the gospel message by being a scribe to Paul, who wrote more New Testament books of the Bible than anyone else. He did all this despite medical issues with his stomach. John the Baptist lived like a wild man out in the wilderness, wore camel's hair, and ate locusts, and that's who Jesus chose to be His front man and announce His coming—not someone in costly king's apparel who smelled clean. Then you've got Moses, who couldn't talk well and stuttered, yet was chosen by God to negotiate with the powerful Pharaoh. He was not only a stutterer but also a murderer, but that's who God chose to deliver the Israelites from 400 years of slavery.

> *Whatever God gave you and however he made you, no one can belay you if God wants to display you*

Do you see from Esther's and Leah's stories, or the little I mentioned about John, Timothy and Moses, that no matter if God made you beautiful or plain, what we're going through, what issues we face or what sins we've committed, God can turn our circumstances around and use them for good?

I want you to know that you can make a difference for generations to come. By being open, willing, and accepting, you allow God to use you for the good of His kingdom, right where you're at, just the way you are. You can be part of making history; you can be part of His-Story.

Who will you reflect?

God created you *on* purpose *for* a purpose, just the way you are. And wouldn't you agree that the highest purpose you could have in life is the purpose God created you for, not what anyone else thinks you should do with your life? You must do what you were born to do. Do you know what that is? On the grand scale, it would be to give Him glory. First Corinthians tells us, "So whether you eat or drink, or whatever you do, do it all for the glory of God" (1 Corinthians 10:31 NLT).

Your purpose on Earth is not merely to know God, to know who He is and try to live the best you can with the revelation you have of Him. Your purpose is more than that: it is to reflect Him.

Are you familiar with how the moon gets its light? The moon doesn't have any light of its own; it's a reflective surface. It is illuminated by the sun shining on it. The more directly the sun shines on it, the more light it has. And like the moon, we also reflect who we've been spending the most time with.

Without God, we're pretty dark, but the more time we spend in His presence, the more He shines on us, the brighter we get. When we align ourselves with Him, we start to reflect Him in our thoughts, words, and deeds. We start to shine like He shines. If the Holy Spirit lives inside us, and we are spending time in God's presence, people should see the characteristics of Christ "lighting us up." We must do more than only have a revelation of who God is, but also reflect Him in all that we do. Our highest goal is that when people look at us, they see Him. Romans tells us our design and purpose are to be conformed to the image of His Son (Romans 8:29). Our purpose in life is similar to the moon's: the moon's purpose is to reflect the sun, and our purpose is to reflect the Son.

And though every single believer has the same purpose in the big picture—we're all called to reflect the Son—you also have an individual purpose that only you yourself, and nobody else, can accomplish. So yes, we should look like Him by

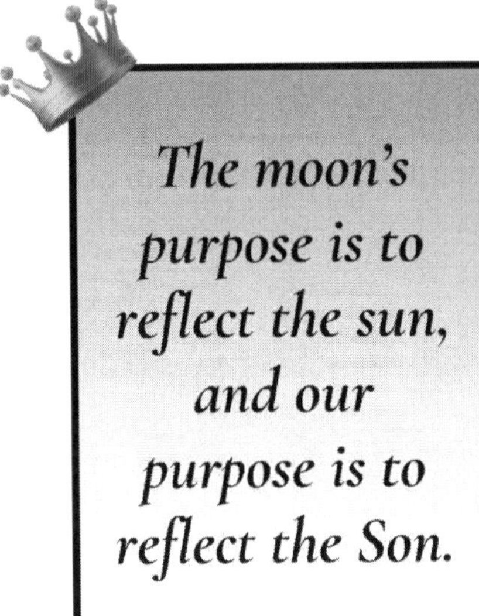

reflecting Him. Plus, He decided to make each of us completely unique, making it impossible to compare ourselves to anyone else. This means our calling and purpose on the more up-close, smaller picture are unlike what anyone else is called to do. No one can do what I do, the way I do it, and the way God purposed for me to do it. And no one can do what you do, the way you do it, and the way God purposed for you to do it.

God gave you your creativity, your different way of looking at things, your specific skill set, and yes, even your looks, to be like nobody else. He decided whether you should be a man or a woman. He chose your height, what color skin and eyes you'd have, and even the texture of your hair. Was He only throwing paint against the proverbial wall, seeing what colors would stick? No. He has a reason for everything He does. He sees beauty in our differences. God knows that if you align with Him and reflect Him back, no matter what you look like on the outside or what your abilities are, you'll shine. You'll succeed in your individual calling. You'll have all His characteristics—love, joy, peace, and wholeness. You'll light up the darkness for others.

What often happens, though, is that if we don't like something about ourselves, we start to think God didn't know what He was doing, or we think He made a mistake when He made us the way He did. We can accuse God of being wrong and question why we are the way we are. But if we wish all day long to be like someone else whom we deem to be better than us, we are slowly backing away from God, our light source, and growing more and more dim. We'll never shine as bright as possible if we're trying to emulate or reflect another human being, even if the rest of the world idolizes them and thinks they're amazing. We can only *live true, love hard and shine bright* if we're reflecting Him.

The way God made you, and the way God does things, may not all make sense to you; you may not comprehend all that He does. But one thing you've got to understand is that His thoughts are not your thoughts, and His ways are not your ways. His ways are much higher (Isaiah 55:8-9). I saw an interview recently with a world-famous actor, and when he was asked the question, "What will you say to God when you get to Heaven?" This actor answered, "God will have a lot of explaining to do." This actor was quite presumptuous to think that he knows better than God and that God is going to owe him an answer.

If you start to question God's ways—when you think, "God has some explaining to do"—when you think you're too fat, too thin, too tall, too small, too dumb, too poor—or perhaps you were born with some deformity, or you have a physical or mental challenge you must overcome, and you think that is what is stopping you from living the life you are meant to live, you'll start to believe He doesn't know what He's doing—as if the God who created you is in total shock how you turned out. That's like thinking He's up in Heaven with an instruction book trying to figure out how to put a human together, the way we do with home furniture that requires self-assembly, and He finds that we have a bunch of screws and washers left over, and He questions the finished product. When you start to think this way, it'll begin to pull you out of your purpose and the destiny He created you for: His design in making you.

> *Live true love hard and shine bright*

I promise you, God was not practicing, and He's not sitting up there now, trying to "figure it out." He didn't make a mistake when He made you. If you believe that something about yourself that you have no control over, whether mentally or physically, is keeping you from what should be—keeping you from your dreams, goals, your calling and your purpose—you're the one who is incorrect, not God.

How can you know for sure that God didn't make a mistake when He made you? You're about to find out.

Chapter Three

You Are God's Favorite Creation

Have you ever felt like there's nothing very good about you? I know I have, like that old saying, "He's got a face only a mother could love." What do they mean when they say that? It seems to suggest that some people are born so ugly, or have so very little going for them, that nobody could love them except the person who gave birth to them. Some of you may not have even known how it felt to have your mother love you. Yet God's love for you goes way beyond the love of even the best mothers on Earth. Isaiah 49:15 (ESV) tells us, "Can a woman forget her nursing child, that she should have no compassion on the son of her womb? Even these may forget, yet I will not forget you." God's telling us that even if our own mother forgets us, He will never forget us. Have you ever taken the time to ponder God's infinite love for you, His desire for your well-being? Jeremiah says, "…I have loved you with an everlasting love; therefore I have continued my faithfulness to you" (Jeremiah 31:3 ESV). In 3 John 2, we're told God wishes above all things that we prosper and be in good health, even as our soul prospers.

If God loves us with an everlasting love and wants everything to turn out good for us, how would you imagine He shows it? If God were to describe you to the angels, what would He say? When something is precious to you, do you smile and light up when talking about it or thinking about it? Do you remember the pride you felt when your child first called you "Mommy" or "Daddy"? God's face lights up every time He thinks of you. If He had a refrigerator, your picture would be on it. He never forgets about you. You are His favorite.

What do you do when something is your favorite? And I'm not even talking about a person, which has way more meaning, but something as simple as, say, a shirt? Your favorite shirt. When something is your favorite, you don't wear it when you're changing the oil in your car; you don't eat a big plate of spaghetti while you have it on because you don't want it to get stained; you keep it safe. You keep it from spills; maybe you have it dry cleaned or hand-wash it. You wear it on special occasions when you want to feel good, not when you're going hiking, because it could get snagged on a branch and torn. That's the care we sometimes take with just a piece of cloth.

Have you ever worked at a job where the boss played favorites? Did he treat certain employees better than he treated others? Or maybe your own parents played favorites with one of your siblings, and did special things for them, took them special places and bought them gifts you never got, and it made you feel inferior?

The thing about God is that He doesn't play favorites with his children that way. When it comes to all the amazing things God created, *you* are His favorite. He likes you better than rainbows, kittens, and sunshine. Have you thought about how you fit into the ranking of all the wonderful things God made? Let's go to Genesis, Chapter 1, to find out what happened during creation and see how you and I fit into the picture.

When God made everything

When the earth was without form and void, and darkness was everywhere, on the first day, God called forth light, and He saw that it was good. The second day, He divided the land from the sea and gave us oceans, and He saw that it was good. The third day, He made all the grass, herbs and delectable fruit, seeds, vegetation, and trees, and He saw that it was good. The fourth day, God put stars in the heavens and the sun and the moon in the sky, to show us the difference between day and night, and He saw that it was good. On the fifth day, God made every creature of the sea, everything that flies in the air—ladybugs, majestic owls, dolphins, starfish, hummingbirds, macaws—all kinds of sea creatures, fish, birds, and insects—and many more. And can you guess what He thought about the fifth day of His creation? He saw that it was good.

And on the sixth day, God made every beast on the land—sleek panthers, furry orangutans, zebras, giraffes, white Bengal tigers, chameleons, your favorite puppy. And do you have any idea what He saw when He looked at His creation? He saw that it was good. *Good.* But … just "good"? That's it?

On that sixth day after He finished making millions of astonishing things … He still wasn't satisfied. Can we even grasp that God just did something more jaw-dropping than painting the equivalent of millions of Sistine Chapels, and it wasn't good enough for Him? God has some high standards. How do we know it wasn't good enough for Him? Because there was one last thing to create before He felt like the earth was complete. How do you fit into that picture? Out of everything God created, we are His crowning creation. The only one made in His image and likeness. The only part of His creation *made like Him,* and the only one given dominion over all the earth (more on what this means to you in my follow-up book, *So I'm Worthy, Now What?*).

> *"So God created man in his own image, in the image of God created he him; male and female created he them. And God blessed them…"* Genesis 1:27-28 (NKJV).

We see each day after God made all the things He made, He said they were good. Yet when you come to verse 31 (NKJV), after He had made the final part of His creation—man in His own image—*"Then God saw everything that He had made, and indeed it was very good."* Are you getting this? Everything He made was good, but after making us, He saw us and said it was VERY good! He did a better job with us than He did with the peacocks, eagles, swans, mandarin fish, Siberian huskies, tigers, the Grand Canyon, Bora Bora Island, the Giant's Causeway, or any other bird, animal, or landscape you think is amazing. Everything else He made was just "good." But you and I are *very* good. *We* are His best creation.

> *"And on the seventh day God ended his work which he had made; and he rested on the seventh day from all his work which he had made. And God blessed the seventh day, and sanctified it: because that in it he had rested from all his work which God created and made"* (Genesis 2:2-3 KJV).

You hear that? After making us, He sat back and rested. He felt no need to make anything else after He made us. He didn't feel the need to do any improving upon us—another version, a better, new and improved version, a version that would just be perfectly obedient and do everything right. He didn't say, "Oh, boy, I really messed up on this one. What was I thinking?" No, He couldn't mess you up; you were made in His image and likeness. Only after creating *us*—you and me—was He able to sit back on His throne, kick His feet up on a stool, and just admire His masterpiece, and finally say, "Drop the mic; I got nothin' after that."

So how can you look at the stunning view of the Grand Canyon, the majesty of the snow-capped mountains, the vastness of the star-filled sky, or a breathtaking sunset and be in awe of that creation, and then look in the mirror at God's *ultimate* creation and say, "I'm unworthy; I'm a piece of junk; I don't deserve to be here; I'm no good"? Are you kidding me? Sure, the beaches and oceans in paradise locations are good, but you, you are *very* good ... just the way you are.

Do not insult your Creator by calling what He made, loves, and cherishes "worthless." Isaiah 45:9 (NLT) reminds us, "Does the clay dispute with the one who shapes it, saying, 'Stop, you're doing it wrong!' Does the pot exclaim, 'How clumsy can you be?'" How can we think we know more than the God who fashioned us and made us just the way we are for a purpose? Philippians 2:13 (NKJV) says, "for it is God who works in you both to will and to do for His good pleasure." Do you know that you give Him pleasure? That He loved you enough to send His Son to die for you while you were still a sinner? And if He did that, how will He not freely give you all things (Romans 8:32), including your dreams? Listen to me: You're worth much more to God than any other creation. The Father didn't send His Son to die for the panda bears, penguins, or bunny rabbits, as cute as they are. He didn't even die for the angels who worship him. He died for you and me in all our imperfections.

You were only meant to be you

I'm here to tell you that, as flawed as you think you might be, there's nothing about you that can stop you from being who God created you to be. There is not a thing besides death (and sometimes not even death) that can stop you from accomplishing the great purpose God put you on Earth to accomplish. And you are worthy of it. You already have everything living inside you to make that happen. But if you become indoctrinated by the world's ways, from everything around you—the examples you see from TV programs, movies, and magazines, and their opinions of what beauty, success, and smarts should look like—and if you take that false ideal and compare yourself, you can never win. When you're trying to fit inside a box society made that God never intended for you to be in, you allow yourself to be trapped. There's no way you can be like those people in the magazines, because even those people in the magazines don't look like those people in the magazines.

I don't know if you're old enough to remember the supermodel Cindy Crawford from the 1990s. I was just a teenager, and I wanted to look like her (forgetting that even if God did a miracle and added four or five inches to my height, it was never going to happen because I'm not her, and I wasn't called to the same purpose she was called to). But still, I tried to eat the way she did, bought her workout video, and did whatever she recommended in magazine articles. It never made me even come close to having her physique.

Then I saw this program on TV that showed what she had to go through to get one great-looking photo to go on the cover of a magazine. Not only did she have to be extremely disciplined in her sleep, eating, water intake, and exercise, but she'd also have a whole team of hair, makeup and wardrobe people spending hours making her look perfect for the photo shoot. She'd have a team of people to make the lighting, scenery, and backdrops flattering, and she had the top photographers to snap her pictures. They'd take several hundred photos, and from several hundred photos, they'd find "the one." After they found the one, they still weren't done. They'd doctor the picture to fix any stray hair, delete any pimple, even out any skin issues, flatten a bloated tummy, and remove any scars, freckles, or cellulite. But what shocked me the most was that even with this tall, thin, toned bombshell, they'd shave the equivalent of about four inches off her hips in the photo. Here I insulted myself, thinking I wasn't worthy because I didn't look like Cindy Crawford, when even Cindy Crawford didn't look like Cindy Crawford (at least not the one on the magazine cover).

You were never made to be like anyone else. We are like snowflakes: no two are ever the same. You're utterly unique, which makes you precious. If you've ever watched a show on antiques or collectibles, you know the rarer something is, the more it is worth. Your individuality is the root of your true beauty, because no one else is like you. Even identical twins, formed from the same split egg, don't share the same fingerprints. You being one of a kind shows how cherished you are. When something is unlike any other, the value for that item is incalculable. Your worth is incalculable. You are priceless.

Likewise, you were never made to look like anyone else but you. Just like I was never supposed to look like Cindy Crawford; the only person I'm supposed to look like besides Katherine Norland is God. I'll explain that later.

If you've ever wondered if life would be better if you did a little cosmetic surgery, or even improved and enhanced your outer package without going under the knife, read on. I'm about to share what type of God-approved approaches you can take to look better and feel better inside and out.

Chapter Four

God-Medic Surgery

If you're like me, one of the things you may be pondering is the immortal query of Shakespeare, who said, "To nip or tuck? That is the question." Er, ah, well, maybe he didn't say that. But it might be what you are thinking about. Now, you may wonder why I'm going to talk about plastic surgery in a book about your worthiness as it's found in Christ. It seems like one of those topics Christians like to ignore or not admit they think about or be vehemently against.

Did you know that according to the American Society of Plastic Surgeons, nearly $16.7 billion was spent on cosmetic procedures in the U.S. in 2020?

I worked on a film set recently, and one of the crew members told me that on a recent trip to Seoul, South Korea, every other billboard he saw was promoting plastic surgery, and there was a plastic surgery clinic on every block. He said he wandered through a hotel lobby and overheard a mother telling her daughter, who appeared to be around 8 or 9 years old, that if she did well on her school test, then Mom would take her to get that nose job. Plastic surgery is so common there that it's been called the plastic surgery capital of the world. There, 60% of women in their 20s have done some cosmetic procedure. That co-worker also said these clinics often have menus, just like a fast-food place has combo meals. You can order a Number 1 for nose; a 2 for nose and eyes; Combo 3 for nose, eyes, and chin; a 4 for nose, eyes, chin and breasts; a 5 for nose, eyes, chin, breasts and butt. The list goes on. It is estimated that 20% of Korean men are also getting plastic surgery.[1]

These procedures are happening more and more frequently all over the world, but not everyone is admitting it or is open to talking about it. Even though millions of people are doing it, it seems to be sort of a taboo topic, mostly for the people who have done it. Perhaps they want to keep the illusion that how they look is all natural. Besides the millions who get cosmetic work done, there are many more millions who think about it. Have you ever wondered what it would be like to have a cosmetic procedure and how it would turn out? Do you have what you consider problem areas you've tried to fix or something you consider a physical flaw, and wonder, "If I just had that thing fixed, made bigger, made smaller, or could freeze the fat off my abs, then life would be better"? Or at the very least, you'd just feel better about yourself? Have you thought about having some work done—even if it's not invasive like a surgery, just some Botox or fillers? Would that make you more competitive in a job market that praises youth, more attractive in the dating world or to your spouse? I know I've thought about these things. I'm an actor, and the entertainment industry is known both for ageism and for judging people, and rewarding them with acting roles or not, based on their looks.

Perhaps there are a few people who get cosmetic surgery who don't have self-worth issues. Yet many people I talk to who have worthiness issues have thought about getting work

---

[1] https://www.townandcountrymag.com/style/mens-fashion/a32057377/male-plastic-surgery-around-the-world/

done. And then many who have are ashamed, unnecessarily, that they did. God encourages us to forget the former things: "Don't even remember them: I'm doing a new thing," He says in Isaiah (vv. 43:18-19). So, let's talk about it just in case it's something you've thought about, considered, had done, or judged others for doing. I promise you, though, this chapter will go much further than skin deep. Soon you'll be able to see yourself and love yourself the way God does, so you'll have the confidence and the courage to go after your God-given dreams.

Life happens to us all

You've read that you are more breathtaking than the sunset, you're God's favorite creation, and you are very good. Yet if we're being honest with ourselves, sometimes even knowing how God feels about us and what matters to Him doesn't change how we view ourselves.

I want you to know you're not alone. When I found out how God felt about me and that I was important to Him, a switch didn't just flip in me automatically to make me love myself and have no doubts, questioning, or comparison. It was an everyday process to renew my mind with the scriptures. It still is, the same way we brush our teeth twice a day, or more if we need it. One thing that helps me is reading the Bible every day and having the audio Bible play in the background at home, sometimes even while I sleep, to wash out all the junk and debris worldly views have planted. That's the best way to build and strengthen your faith. As Romans 10:17 tells us, "So then faith comes by hearing, and hearing by the word of God" (NKJV). I had to continually hear what God had to say about me to know who I was and how much value I had. His opinion is really the only one that matters.

When I bring up the topic of wanting to change our looks and improve them, I know a few of you may think, "This chick has no idea what I look like or what I'm going through, how bad I've got it or how hard my life's been. I bet she's never had to deal with any of the rejection issues I've had to deal with. I see her picture on the book. She's got it all together; she doesn't have anything wrong with her; she looks fine; she's a Hollywood actress. She wouldn't know what it's like to have people ask you in public if you're pregnant when you're not. Or when you go out with your buddies, have people think you're their parent instead of their friend; what it's like never to have gone on a date before, or to be disfigured from birth or an accident. She doesn't know what it's like to have your children hate you, to have your husband leave you for someone else, or to be paralyzed."

Perhaps someone may have told you in your formative years that you were a terrible singer, so you never sang again. Or you weren't good at art, so even though it was your passion, you let it go. You may be riddled with anxiety, and you can't leave the house, or you've never taken a chance because you're afraid to fail. Or whatever it is that has you hung up right now. And you're right, I don't know what you look like, what you've been through, or what kind of ridicule you've had to face.

People assume things about others that aren't true. I know people have judged you based on your outer package and what they thought that said about you, and they were way off. Just like when I struggled to pay rent working in a factory on an assembly line, and another co-worker questioned me, asking what I was doing there because she said I "looked rich." (I was living in a trailer park. Yeah, that's rich.) Somehow people think they can tell your financial status from genetics you had nothing to do with. But no matter what we look like on the outside, whether we feel it's a blessing or a curse, and even whether we love the Lord or not, there's one thing I know: We've all dealt with loss, betrayal, disappointment, and rejection. "The rain falls on the just and the unjust alike" (Matthew 5:45). No matter who you are, you're sometimes going to deal with bad situations in life.

Though I don't know what you've been through, what your hang-ups are, or what you look like, I know we all have our own journey we must work through. What I've been through may be nothing compared to what you have.

The sad part for me at the time was, I still let my experience stop me, and keep me from my calling. I believed those who put me down and told me I was nothing and I'd never make it. I allowed what I went through, no matter how insignificant it may seem to those of you who've been through unbelievable tragedies, to derail the plans God had for me.

You see, I've been more than 80 pounds heavier than I am now, busting out of my husband's sweatpants, my swollen elephant feet not fitting into men's extra-large flip-flops. At one point, I had such bad acne that people would lose their appetite for pizza when I walked into the room (I was accused of having meningitis). I've been made fun of because of my two different colored eyes. Even my own talent manager called me a "Barnum and Bailey Circus freak." I've had directors grab and squeeze my muffin top, or backhand me in the stomach, and say, "Lose this, or you're not on the show." I've had hundreds of other judgments and insults hurled at me by executives in the entertainment industry and others who thought I wasn't good enough. I was a late bloomer, tormented for being "flat as a board." Let me tell you, half-empty cups are no hope chest. I believed I was worthless and hideous, and no one would ever want to be my friend. I'd cry myself to sleep at night until my pillowcases became a Petri dish of mascara and snot.

I understand what it's like to be miserable, to hate myself so much I was convinced nobody would miss me if I was gone.

When giving up is interrupted

I grew up in a trailer park in the middle of a vast cornfield called Minnesota. I never thought I'd amount to anything. My aspirations weren't those of becoming a star in Tinseltown; my dreams were of tinfoil … which covered the cardboard guitar I made for the school talent show.

My ladder of success was a real ladder spackled in paint that I'd climb on Saturdays to paint houses with my dad. My dad once sat us down and said we didn't have money to buy condiments anymore for our mystery-meat hot dogs. Goodbye Mr. Ketchup; see you later Mrs. Mustard; et tu, my savory mayonnaise friend. That level of poverty didn't bother me, but the non-stop bullying did. Popular kids judged me by the labels on my back. Or, in my case, the lack thereof. Shopping at thrift stores was not considered cool; it was a dirty secret you tried to hide.

But there was one thing the rich and popular kids couldn't take away from me, and that was the joy I felt doing the high school talent shows. Nearly every show I directed and acted in, I won top prize. I finally felt like I'd found something I was good at, and it didn't matter where I grew up and how much I didn't have. I was creating; I was happy. I'd discovered my dream. For the first time, I felt like I'd succeeded. But it was high school; it didn't last.

I moved to a new town. I could start over in the big city. Granted, it was only 10 miles away from home. I went from a town of 9,000 to a town of 40,000. Here, no one knew I was a loser. No one knew I was the kid forced to wear the green corduroy slacks in the nurse's office whenever I couldn't make it to the bathroom because I was that kid who constantly peed her pants at South Elementary.

Now, I was 18, living on my own in a "poor man's high rise." Let's be honest, it was a complex of single-wide trailers stacked on top of each other. But bigger towns spawn bigger bullies. My dreams were pummelled by naysayers. I stopped believing in those dreams and started just existing. I had no job, no money, no car, no TV, no phone, and no boyfriend. Surviving on ramen noodles and Pig's Eye beer. After a fight with really my only friend, I was ashamed, humiliated, and hurting so badly that I stopped believing life was worth living.

I was starring in my own Nordic novella. On a humid summer night as black as tar, sweat pouring down my face faster than the tears, all I could think of was wanting to stop the pain. My palms were sweaty, but I managed to lock the bathroom door. With my still moist fingertips, I fumbled with the childproof cap of my prescription. I was heaving with anxiety, determined that tonight would be the last night I'd feel pain again. I recited a poem to myself:

"You have no one who loves you; you have no one who cares,
And even if you cry for help, no one is really there.
Your life is empty, meaningless; you never will be strong,
When all the world's against you, why bother going on?"

Then I swallowed an entire bottle of Prozac.

I stumbled out of my four-story trailer high rise and into the streets. I don't know where I ended up or how far I got. I didn't even think to leave a note. I didn't know where I was when I blacked out. The unknown man who found me could have done anything to me. Instead, I woke up in an Emergency Room strapped to a table, gagging on a tube forcing charcoal into my stomach.

I was angry, and cursing out the medical staff. Those idiots were trying to save me. Didn't they know it was a waste of their time, that I was a lost cause, a waste of space? Didn't they know they were ruining my plans? For at least one day, I was going to be famous, and on the cover of the newspaper. There are two ways I could have been memorialized: They could have written about my death as a murder victim by the strange man who found me, or a suicide.

But that's not what was written.

Nobody knows what another person has gone through. God saved me that day. He wants to save you. You may think the story of your life is over, that it's already written, that it has a bad ending, and there's no hope for you. But God isn't finished with your book yet. He's not finished with you. He wants to empower you, like He did me, to pick up your pen and be in charge of your own destiny.

So … how will you write your next chapter?

Chapter Five

Learning to Love Myself

You read about what happened when I took my first acting class, and how looking in the mirror triggered my sadness and depression in life more than any other event.

I couldn't face who I was. Yet somehow, through prayer and reading the word of God, I was able to get over my fears long enough to take a chance and move to Los Angeles. I made this brave move because I felt God was calling me to be an actress and moving to L.A. was being obedient to Him. But when I moved to Los Angeles, I wore a lot of masks. I covered up who I really was and how I felt about myself.

On one occasion, at an entertainment industry networking event at a swanky hotel, I dressed the part of an ingenue. I had on my smiling, confident, happy mask as I floated around the room and tried to make contacts that might lead to acting roles. I met a Hollywood talent manager named Marshall Ferguson, who, after only a couple of moments exchanging small talk and pleasantries, stared me in the eyes and asked me, "Why do you hate yourself so much?"

That question shook me to my core. Here I was, almost 2,000 miles from that acting class in Minneapolis. No one else knew that I hated myself and couldn't even stand to look in the mirror. Yet this stranger somehow knew my secret—one I hadn't repeated since that painful day years before. I don't know how many hours we talked that day and the days that followed, but God sent him into my life to be the mentor and coach I needed to begin the process of shaking me out of my low self-worth issues.

Within the first week of meeting Marshall, he gave me two extremely difficult assignments. One, which is not unheard of in this industry, was to take a picture of myself in a bikini and send it to him, which I was mortified to do. But if you're considered a pretty young thing in Hollywood, agents and managers need to see their "product" to know how to pitch them for jobs.

Sometimes facing your fear is the only way to get over it. Even worse than that first assignment (if you can imagine anything worse than that) was the second one, because it involved me confronting what I thought was my biggest enemy: the mirror.

What he told me I had to do every day for the next two weeks was stand in front of the mirror naked and say, "I love you," to the person staring back at me. And yes, I had to do it with the lights on. I stood there, becoming familiar with everything about myself I didn't like, that I thought was wrong, unproportionate, chubby, bulging, misshapen, or scarred. And I had to repeat over and over, "I love you," and keep saying it each day until I believed it.

Sometimes facing your fear is the only way to get over it

That exercise was not easy for me. Many years later, I

learned the truth about where my problems with my value and worth really came from at their core. They weren't about what my earth suit actually looked like; my problems stemmed from how I felt about myself, regardless of or despite what my outer shell looked like.

Most likely, this is the bind you're in as well.

Hot does not equal happy

For a lot of people, worthiness issues spring up in those who don't have any major physical flaws. I've seen the same thing happen with girls who would be considered super-hot.

I have two female friends who look like models, who hate how they look. One of them was complaining to me about her nose, asking me whether or not she should get a nose job. I was stunned, because after all the years I'd known her, I never noticed anything wrong with her nose, not in the slightest. Even after she pointed out what she felt was her "trouble area," I didn't see anything that needed fixing. But somehow, she did. She believed the lies whispered in her ear by the deceiver telling her she didn't measure up.

I've had multiple friends, believers and nonbelievers alike, who've had cosmetic procedures done. But one friend in particular, an aspiring singer, has gone under the knife a few times, and though she looks like a swimsuit model, she isn't happy with herself or how she looks. When you compliment her, she deflects the compliment and complains about how awful she looks, pointing out her flaws in case you missed them. Though she's spent hundreds of thousands of dollars trying to improve her looks, it never seems to be enough.

For the record, I'm not condemning cosmetic surgery, although I've come to learn that many Christians do. They feel that having any "work done" is just about the worst thing you could do, as you would be grossly sinning against God.

They say the only reason anyone should ever get a procedure done solely for looks is a reconstructive one after having your skin melted from a fire, or if your face goes through a windshield in a car accident; or you've had cancer and a mastectomy and your breasts are removed, only then is it okay to replace them.

They say things like, "Well, if God wanted you to look like that, He would have made you look like that." But you can't really apply that logic all the way either, because then why would you even wear clothes? If He wanted you to wear clothes, you would have been born with them on. Or if He wanted your fingernails short, He would have designed them not to grow.

How would you get computer work done with nails that were a foot long? There are some things that just happen from our fallen nature that were not part of God's original intent or His design for us. Hence the fig leaf outfits, which turned into animal skins and evolved into linen, wool, cashmere, and polyester. And hey, now we've got Spandex, and I'm almost positive Spanx are an invention that came down from the heavenlies.

But think about it: Without the fall of mankind in the garden due to sin, we probably wouldn't be wearing clothes right now. Without Eve eating the fruit, would we have discovered lip gloss, laser hair removal, or liposuction? Maybe? Maybe not?

Religion is for reverence, not condemnation

If your mind were continually fixed on Jesus, the author and finisher of your faith, your looks wouldn't be a concern to you. But here you are living in this fallen world, and God gave you free will to choose what you do with your life, which includes how you look.

Yet a word of caution should be said here. Sometimes people make up false doctrines using what God never said in the Bible, or they take what was said out of context and misconstrue its meaning, putting a heavy burden on people or shaming those who don't follow it.

The Old Testament laws are not what we are under anymore; we are under God's grace (Romans 6:14). When God gave us the laws in the Old Testament to follow, they weren't meant to be a burden to us; they were meant to be a gift, to show us how to please God with our lifestyle.

They were one way God's people would be set apart from those who didn't know God. (I teach more about how we can live in a way that pleases God in my upcoming book and course, *You Are Loved*.)

Religion should be in place to help us show reverence and honor God, not condemn people. Yet here in America, there are religious organizations that don't allow you to wear makeup or to dance. Or they tell you you've got to wear skirts below your knees, even down to your ankles, and have your hair a certain length or always have your hair covered.

Those things in and of themselves aren't bad; they might even be considered praiseworthy or prudent in a certain context or situation. But when the religious laws become more important than the heart of God or showing people God's love, we've missed it; we've missed God's heart and His intent to draw people to Him, and instead, we are pushing them away by our stringent behavior.

Do I think people shouldn't wear makeup, or color their hair? Absolutely not. Do I think God is concerned or upset if we do? No. He's less concerned about your outer appearance. He's most concerned about the contents of your heart.

But for now, I want to work from the outside in. Because I know when dealing with worthiness issues, a lot of it stems from our perception of how we look, or comments made by others about how we look.

Scripture tells us, "...man looks at the outward appearance, but the LORD looks at the heart" (1 Samuel 16:7b AMP).

Do you know what the scriptures have to say about your looks? There's a lot to discuss when it comes to our appearance. Let's get into why fixing the outside won't help an inside problem.

Chapter Six

Fixing the Outside Won't Help an Inside Problem

If you were in real estate trying to sell a house, would planting flowers beside the walkway make it more appealing? How about putting new shingles on the roof and replacing cracked windows? It would, right? When something looks nice on the outside, it has in real estate what's called "curb appeal." But no matter how good it looks on the outside, when the appraiser does a deep dive into the property, they'll know if your walls are full of rats chewing electrical wires or termites eating away at the wood, or your foundation is cracked. Will your home's value be what you hope it will? No, it would be crazy to think it would.

In the same way, you must stay out of the trap of thinking that sprucing up your body and giving it some "curve appeal" by getting liposuction or a butt lift is going to heal the hole in your heart or make you feel like you have more value when you're being eaten away on the inside and when what you're building and basing your life on has a cracked foundation (things that don't matter to God in light of eternity or your calling).

If you don't appreciate and value who you are now, the way God made you, then doing anything to your exterior isn't going to make a lasting impact on your view of yourself. There's no amount of cosmetic work you can get done (or do to yourself) that will change that or make you happy. It will be empty and hollow. Many come to find only disappointment in this awful truth:

> *"Although they've had a nip and tuck,*
> *their worth is down, and life still sucks."*

Those who think fixing the outside is the answer, that if they just look a certain way then they will be worthy and other people will love them, often find after they've changed their appearance that nothing significant happens for them. You may get a little more attention and compliments and feel a bit more confident … for a season. But if you never take care of what is on the inside, never make peace with who you are, you will keep searching to fill that emptiness. Your unhappiness will return, and you may go back under the knife again, because you can't use an outward solution for an inward problem.

We've become a society bent on quick fixes in a bottle. Have you ever seen a commercial for men's cologne or deodorant? Within 30 seconds, they make you believe that by using a couple of spritzes or swipes of their product, scantily clad supermodels will be swarming you like mosquitoes in the bayou. But if a man who has trouble finding a girlfriend hasn't taken care of what is going on inside him, not even truckloads of the product will garner him the attention of a woman. And on the other hand, someone who has taken care of the fixes they need on the inside, or at least is working on them, could attract a woman they'd want to spend their life with even if they bathed in skunk oil.

I have an acquaintance in her 80s who has had a myriad of cosmetic procedures done and wanted to do more, but her doctor finally told her she would not be allowed to have any more elective surgeries at her age, because it could be dangerous. For some people, the desperation to look a certain way is something you don't outgrow even as you mature, even if you may be putting your life at risk. Once you've had a procedure, it's very tempting to keep going back and doing more.

I wrote on the topic of how to see yourself the way God sees you in my book *Poetic Prescriptions for Eternal Youth: Examining Earthly Beauty from a Heavenly Perspective.* Here are just a couple of lines from that book on this topic:

"Cause once you find a flaw to fix, up pops another one;
When fighting time and gravity, the war is never won."

Another passage says:

"Some folks will do 'most anything;
To keep what's left of youth, they'll cling.
But I'd at 80 be a joke
If looking 30 when I croak.

Say "Yes" to Jesus and you'll gain
A youngness that your age can't change.
With God doth come sound surgery
Where youth's obtained eternally.

I wrote that book only after I'd come to terms with who I was in God's eyes. When I aligned myself with His thoughts, believing them to the point that it shifted my mindset—moved from my head to my heart—then even my behavior changed. And if you, too, are living in a dark pit of self-hatred, like I'd been for years, I want to show you how to get out of it.

Getting to the heart of the matter

Scripture says, "Therefore we do not lose heart, but though our outer man is decaying, yet our inner man is being renewed day by day" (2 Corinthians 4:16 NASB)—or at least our inner man should be renewed, and it will be if we keep working on it and building up our spirit. This verse tells us that we can lose heart if we aren't allowing our spiritual side to grow, and if we are only focused on this decaying flesh (which, let's be honest, is not getting any better but will soon be back in the dust it was made from). We can get depressed and feel terrible about life.

You may be thinking, *Okay, I get it; fixing the outside won't help an inside problem. Then what do I do? Especially if I don't like myself, and I can't find any reasons to like myself? I'm lonely. No one loves me, but at least if I looked better, it might make me happy because people would pay attention to me instead of ignoring me.* Or maybe you've got some other variation for why you want to lose weight or bulk up at the gym or do some drastic measure to attain a certain aesthetic.

If you haven't gotten down to the root of your worthiness issues—why you really think you're not good enough, don't measure up, or aren't as valuable as others—then doing all those things to improve your outside is basically the same thing as treating a symptom rather than what's causing the symptoms.

A symptom is a sign or indication that something is going on; it's evidence that there's some sort of occurrence, like one that accompanies a particular disease. My son, Timothy, has allergies, and before I learned what the root cause was, he would sneeze a lot, have red itchy eyes, and his face and neck would break out with a rash. I'd give him allergy pills for these symptoms. But the sneezing, red eyes, and rash weren't the problem; it only seemed like they were. After further investigation, it turned out he was allergic to cats. Cats were the root of the problem. Once we were able to keep him away from cats and not visit our friends' houses who had cats, he no longer needed the allergy medicine.

Similarly, the things you don't like about yourself aren't stopping you from living the life you want to live; it only seems like they are. The real problem is the root: You actually don't love yourself enough just the way you are, which is why you wonder if fixing certain things about you will make you like yourself.

If you spray it, they will come

To show you how you can apply this to your life with whatever issues you might have with knowing your worth, let's go back to the guy who thinks if he just wears the cologne from the commercial, he'll attract women. Let's say this man has faced all kinds of rejection in his life: women don't look at him, and when he's tried to look at them and smile in the past, he's seen that they don't smile back, or they turn away. Perhaps in the past, he's tried to be kind to a woman and open the door for her, and she got upset. So now, when he goes out, he keeps to himself. He keeps his head down. If a woman notices he's looking at her, he quickly averts his eyes. He doesn't look for opportunities to reach out and be kind because he wants to spare himself the disapproval he received in the past. He's told himself a story that women don't like him and aren't attracted to him. Now he keeps his posture closed off, subconsciously. He doesn't even know he's doing this as a way of protecting himself from rejection.

But then let's say he buys a bottle of this cologne. He believed what he saw on the commercials about its ability to attract women, and even his buddies have said, "Man, if you wear this cologne, the girls won't be able to keep their hands off you!" The guy combs his hair, puts his favorite shirt on, and sprays on a few spritzes of the fragrance. He feels good, knowing this has worked for others, and it's going to work for him. He's a little nervous, but he thinks, *Hey, it really worked for the guys in those commercials.* He heads out with his shoulders back, his head held high, not looking at the ground anymore. He's got a smile on his face and a skip in his step.

He sees a woman. She smiles and notices him, and because his head is up, he sees she gives him a little smile and a nod. Then he smiles and nods back at her; his face blushes a little, and BAM!—he gets a dopamine hit. Now he feels even better. His heart beats a little faster, and his confidence grows.

(A little on dopamine, from *Psychology Today:* "Dopamine is known as the feel-good neurotransmitter. It's a chemical that ferries information between neurons. The brain releases it when we eat food that we crave or while we have sex, contributing to feelings of pleasure and satisfaction as part of the reward system.")

The next woman he looks at, he smiles even more. She smiles back and does a little giggle because she's not had many bold men smile at her broadly like this, and she doesn't know what to do. His confidence grows a little more, and now he's not consumed with his inadequacies and isn't thinking about anything that's wrong with him, because he believes this cologne has made him irresistible. He goes into a market and thinks, *I'm going to go for it, I'm going to talk to a woman. It doesn't matter all the times I got turned down in the past because I've got my magic elixir on!*

He sees a pretty woman who can't get something off a high shelf. A strong, capable, confident version of himself shows up. He's become a superhero! Captain High Shelf Reacher to the rescue. He flies in to save the day. He's closer to a woman than he's ever been. He's not going the other direction in the market like he used to, or taking another path. He's right in there helping her pull the cereal box from the shelf. He leans in and hands her the Frosted Flakes, and she takes a deep breath. Now he knows she got a nice big whiff of his cologne. She smiles and thanks him, and suddenly he feels emboldened. He doesn't see a ring on her finger. He strikes up a conversation with her, and after a couple of moments of chit-chat, where she doesn't walk away, yell at him, or throw coffee in his face, he realizes, *With this cologne on, I can't lose!* He asks her to coffee, and she actually says yes! Oh, my goodness, he rushes home to order a lifetime supply of this fragrance.

Let me ask you, was the cologne a magic potion for attracting women? Or is the truth that because he thought he couldn't lose with this fragrance on, he changed his behavior, the way he carried himself, his reactions, his confidence, and his interactions with people? He went out into the world expecting to win instead of expecting to lose; he put himself out there in a way he'd never done before. He saw himself differently, which made others around see him differently.

But remember the other half of the lesson also: Cologne Guy doomed himself to eventual failure (again), because he missed the point completely and avoided the inner issues of what was making him feel bad about himself in the first place. In fact, he was setting himself up for inevitable disappointment down the road—maybe even by the end of that first date. (I mean, what if they go swimming and the scent wears off? Panic alert!)

It's important to recognize that if he doesn't get to the heart of the matter of what makes him feel bad about himself in the first place, his new strategy will eventually fail, leaving him right back where he was. Like the outward things you may have tried to improve how you feel, you eventually find the potions stop working, and you start searching for the next temporary fix.

The appearance of having it all together

If you've had any cosmetic procedures done, I want you to know you don't have to feel bad about it or condemn yourself for it. "There is therefore now no condemnation to them which are in Christ Jesus, who walk not after the flesh, but after the Spirit" (Romans 8:1 KJV).

Also, I'm guessing that if you've done some work to fix your outside, it probably didn't fix the things you wanted it to fix, since you're reading this book. It's like the home I mentioned earlier. You can give it a paint job and new shutters, but if your inner house is being eaten away by termites, it's going to come crashing to the ground. The first thing you've got to do is get an exterminator for your soul to remove the bugs and vermin and yucky thoughts in your mind, which is exactly what I did. It does no good to have your house—your earth suit—look good on the outside while it's uninhabitable on the inside.

I was in that place for years, and I couldn't live like that anymore. I was paralyzed by my pain, but nobody knew. I was grateful to have learned about journaling. Writing down my feelings about life, my hopes for my acting career, and all the ways I felt like I wasn't enough provided relief. If I hadn't had a place to channel those emotions, I might have imploded.

People often have a misconception that if you *look* like you have it all together, then you probably do.

One time, I performed for a casting director at a workshop. I did an intense, gritty scene I thought would show my acting skills and the depths to which I could go. When I finished, he said, "That was really great. I loved it. I believed it. But you'd never get cast in a role like that." I said, "Why not?" He said, "Because pretty people don't have problems." I said, "But Nicole Kidman played the role in the movie, and she's beautiful." He said, "That's because she's Nicole Kidman." Because she's famous, she gets to play whatever roles she wants. The rest of us play whatever roles we're offered until we're famous enough to decide which roles we play.

He went on to say, "You'll only be cast in roles they think would convey the right message they want to tell the audience, based on your essence and how you appear." This particular casting person, and perhaps many others, believed that pretty people didn't have problems. I wish I could have given him a list of mine at the time. The devil doesn't leave you alone just 'cause you're cute.

I've learned from my own experiences that fixing the outside rather than the inside is empty. It doesn't get to the heart of the matter. It leaves you hollower than before, because what you think is going to be the answer to solve your self-worth issues doesn't have the power to do it. You may have learned this too.

Whenever you're feeling bad about yourself—something isn't working in your life, or you feel compelled to handle a situation the way the world would, to treat the symptom rather than the root cause—to "put on the cologne" rather than deal with how you feel about yourself—then you know something is out of alignment, and you've got to get that God connection mended.

Sometimes those exquisitely dressed, impeccable-looking, dripping-with-diamonds people are the most broken.

After I created all the content for *You Are Worthy,* I realized that though many people were having amazing breakthroughs, some were still being held back by things from their past—things that stopped them from fully believing and receiving the life-changing message of their worth. Because of that, I created a solution to help those of you who still feel worthless, like you're a lost cause; who've possibly had some trauma you can't let go of, or you've just got a nagging voice that keeps telling you you'll never be "enough," and you don't know how to stop it.

I want you to finally get free from that. I decided not to add that additional solution to this book because I didn't want it to end up 300 pages long. I wanted to save you time and get the *You Are Worthy* message to you quickly. If the above sounds like something you're struggling with, though, I'll tell you more about that solution in the next chapter.

But first, we need to talk about WHY we feel it's so important to look good, and how God fits into the picture. Let's examine earthly beauty from a heavenly perspective. And why it's better to be holy than hot.

Chapter Seven

The Pursuit of Hotness

I ended the last chapter by saying, "It's better to be holy than hot." When you read that, you might have thought, *What?! Yeah, right, it's better to be holy than hot? Maybe if you're a monk, or a nun, or a shaman. Not where I'm from. People judge you by how you look.* And you're right; people do. "Lookism" is prevalent. That's when you face prejudice or discrimination based on your outer appearance. In many cases, it seems like if you're not hot, you miss out on job opportunities, people won't date you, and nobody will follow you on social media.

Being hot has many benefits. Years' worth of psychological research shows that people with good looks are treated differently. Not only do people who are physically attractive get paid better, but people find them more interesting, and they are assumed to have positive qualities, be more intelligent, and have better social skills.[2]

You might have heard of the "halo effect"? That's what it's called when you view those who are attractive as having positive personality traits based on their looks—people perceive those with better looks to be happier, better parents, more generous and stable, and much more.[3]

---

[2] https://www.vice.com/en/article/gvezeq/the-agony-and-the-ecstasy-of-being-incredibly-hot

[3] https://www.psychologytoday.com/us/blog/habits-not-hacks/201412/the-surprising-power-beautiful-face

Yet Leo Tolstoy said, "It is amazing how complete is the delusion that beauty is goodness."

Think of how many handsome, charming narcissists have ruined people's lives. Satan disguises himself as an angel of light to deceive us (2 Corinthians 11:14).

The devil's beauty was a point of pride for him and played into his fall from grace. "Your heart was proud because of your beauty; you corrupted your wisdom for the sake of your splendor. I cast you to the ground…" (Ezekiel 28:17 ESV). Your looks certainly get you nowhere in Heaven, especially if they elicit pride in you. Yet here on Earth, they make it sound like hotness is our highest calling. (Well, at least if we want to please people and get ahead by earthly standards.)

Hotness is something I strived to have for years. There was a time when I wouldn't ever be caught in public without makeup. In a poem from my book *Poetic Prescriptions for Eternal Youth*, I wrote:

In outward transformation, I'm devout,
Yet restoration's best from inside out...
I'd never been more marvelous to see
Than when I let the Lord make over me...
When we have dropped ourselves and put on Him
We'll shine so bright wherever we were dim.

And it's true. All the stuff I did to make my outside look better paled in comparison to my work on beautifying my inner person. Sure, I got more notice when I was all dolled up and looking good, but nothing lasting came from it. There were fleeting moments of happiness, but not the perpetual joy that comes from a makeover of the soul that only God can give us.

Beauty rewards

I understand the pull to strive to be more beautiful. We're attracted to things of beauty; we're wired that way. There's nothing wrong with having beauty or "being hot"—as long as that's not what you make your life about. But you might be thinking that's all that's important. It's easy to think that way in a society that seems to reward hotness above all else.

Where would certain social media platforms be if there weren't super-hot people who were famous for being, well, "super-hot"? Some celebrities get paid thousands of dollars by clothing companies just to show up at a party for half an hour wearing one of their dresses and having photos taken in it. People get sponsors and get paid lots of money to look good.

Years ago, it seemed like you only had to be hot if you were a model or a movie star. Now it seems like the average everyday person is expected to look like a supermodel. But when we compare ourselves to ideals we'll never be able to meet, it's depressing.

I was watching this influencer on Instagram who was pregnant at the same time I was expecting my second child, and just a week after she had had her baby, she was posing in a sports bra with a flat washboard stomach and hips that didn't look like anything was pushed through them. Meanwhile, I was huge and bloated, heavier than my husband. I couldn't even fit into my maternity clothes. Comparing your journey to someone else's can wreak havoc on your self-esteem.

But do you know what I discovered? *You can't cherish the unique beauty God gave you if you're busy comparing yourself against all the things you're not.*

Being hot is marketable, and all eyes are on you if you are. Sometimes I'm on a video pouring my heart out on a topic I think will help the greatest amount of people, but it doesn't get as many views if I'm in a T-shirt with no makeup on and my hair not done. And I've seen ten times the number of people watching a video where I'm all made up, even if what I'm saying isn't as important.

It's like this new declaration our country has made, and the whole world has made, but it's a Declaration of Dependence, not independence. It says, "We hold these Truths to be self-evident, that all Men are created *unequal,* that they are *reduced* by *Society's Standards* with certain unalienable Rights, that among these are *Death, Enslavement,* and the *Pursuit of Hotness."*

You can't cherish the unique beauty God gave you if you're busy comparing yourself against all the things you're not.

Is the pursuit of hotness worth all the other trappings that come with it, that lead us astray? These are things like unhealthy relationships with food, our bodies, and others; our dependence on compliments, likes, and products; and spending entire paychecks on facials, treatments, personal trainers, and nutritional supplements. I know. I've been there; I've done it. Here in L.A., even some cashiers at the grocery stores wear full glamour makeup and big fake spider eyelashes, like they're going out to a club rather than scanning your beans and broccoli.

Though the pursuit of hotness is not a new phenomenon, now more than ever, there's incentive. Being hot can be monetized on social media with content creation and brand deals. (And who knows, that cashier could get discovered in that checkout line. It worked for Lana Turner and the *Terminator* 2 kid. And basically no one else, ever. But, hey!)

Beauty punishes

Hundreds of people, if not thousands, have been caught pretending to be someone they're not on social media, whether photoshopping their hips smaller or biceps bigger, adding fake abs, or lying about their eye color. When I was researching these imposters, I came across the term "Blackfishing," and I found a few examples of white men and women enhancing their lips and actually dying their skin to appear as if they were Black. I'd never heard of this and was surprised to find multiple instances of it. They were pretending to be someone they were not to get more notice.

We've been conforming for centuries to what the consensus says is hot. Though the people mentioned above wanted to be seen as someone who was blessed with a lot more pigment in their skin, there were long periods of time when people would lighten their skin. The reason for this was that if you had a tan, it would look like you worked outside in the field and didn't have money. To look wealthy, you'd stay out of the sun, making sure it didn't appear like you had to work for a living. Victorian women would even paint their skin with corrosive lead-based enamel paint to look whiter.

To achieve a tiny waist, corsets would be tied so tight a woman couldn't breathe, which would make her pass out. This practice was commonplace enough that a piece of furniture was even invented for these breath-deprived ladies, called a "fainting couch." To have the appearance of fresh, dewy eyes, women would even put the poisonous belladonna plant in their eyes, and it caused blindness!

The obsession with attaining perfection is strong enough for some that they risk killing themselves to do it.

About a hundred people die each year getting cosmetic procedures that don't even need to be done.

Striving to have the perfect body can be dangerous. "It's estimated that 8 million Americans have an eating disorder … The mortality rate associated with anorexia nervosa is 12 times higher than the death rate of ALL causes of death for females 15-24 years old … 20% of people suffering from anorexia will prematurely die from complications related to their eating disorder, including suicide and heart problems … Only 1 in 10 people with eating disorders receive treatment." Listen to this: "80% of 13-year-olds have attempted to lose weight"![4]

What are we doing as a society, by our own behaviors and by what the press and media push, that makes young girls who are just starting to develop and go through puberty think they need to diet when they are in a growing phase? Sometimes the pressure to be accepted is daunting. It can seem that if we look

---

[4] https://www.state.sc.us/dmh/anorexia/statistics.htm

a certain way, we'll be more likely to attract friends and lovers. I knew the feeling all too well when the boys in high school would taunt me for not being developed, calling me a pirate's dream. Yeah, you guessed it, a sunken chest.

Yet the idea of beauty is ever-changing. In the 1960s, a model named Twiggy was popular, and everyone at the time wanted to look super-lean and thin. The modeling industry has been chastised for requiring underweight models. "The average international runway model has a body mass index under 16—low enough to indicate starvation by the World Health Organization's standard." "France passed a law setting lower limits for models' weight [i.e., reducing the threshold necessary to be regarded as unacceptably underweight]. Agents and fashion houses who hire models with a BMI under 18 could pay $82,000 in fines and spend up to six months in jail. Israel also has BMI restrictions for models, and local initiatives regulate models in Milan and Madrid. Those bans were imposed in 2006, after the high-profile deaths of two models."[5]

The modeling industry didn't want these restrictions. But those restrictions the industry thought were unreasonable meant that at a BMI of 18, a 5'9" model would only have to weigh 122 pounds. To put this into perspective, the average female in America is five inches shorter and nearly 50 pounds heavier than this (5'4" and 170.6 pounds).[6]

---

[5] https://www.npr.org/sections/health-shots/2015/12/22/460682633/is-it-time-to-set-weight-minimums-for-the-fashion-industry

[6] https://www.healthline.com/health/womens-health/average-height-for-women

The standards for beauty are always changing. When I was younger, people would tell me I had a big behind. I was insulted by it because that meant I was fat. Now it's in style, and people are getting implants put in their backsides to make their butts more pronounced.

What's more important than how you look is how you feel about yourself. Here's the thing: What people think is hot now may not be tomorrow. Opinions change. Your look may not be in style today, but it could be tomorrow. Remember when freckles were covered up, and teeth with gaps were fixed? Now both are celebrated. There are beauty tricks where people who don't have freckles are now putting them on their faces.

Beauty is subjective

There are many different types of beauty, and many cultures that have any number of opinions on what beauty is. Even men these days are feeling pressured to look more masculine, to have six-pack abs and be the alpha male type who has muscles popping out of his muscles.

In America, for the most part, we love women to be thin in the middle and have an hourglass shape with a pronounced chest and butt. I have a female acquaintance who is obese by American standards and says guys don't even look at her here. But when she was traveling in different countries for ministry work, she had several marriage proposals from men because they love heavier women in those places. If you're not starving but larger, it symbolizes wealth, since (presumably) you have enough money to overeat.

The standards of beauty are different everywhere you go, and sometimes even in the same place in different time periods.

Stick-thin supermodels may be popular now, but there was a period of history when all the women in all the paintings were Rubenesque, when plump ladies with rounded bellies and rolls of soft flesh were considered beautiful and desirable.

There are tribes that find it beautiful or majestic if you have a long neck, so they stretch their necks, one ring at a time. Others find it appealing to stretch their ear lobes or bottom lips out and make large openings in them. Some cultures are still binding girls' and women's feet in unnatural ways because tiny feet are attractive to them.

With these different standards of beauty in different cultures, and the many ways we obtain that beauty, I sometimes wonder why we think our opinions on attractiveness are right and others are wrong. I also wonder why we judge someone's outer appearance at all and say God is pleased with this, but He isn't pleased with that. Are our ways of obtaining beauty better than their ways of obtaining beauty, when God made each and every one of us just the way we are, and didn't feel the need to improve our aesthetics, but rather suggests we work on our souls instead?

With that in mind, there's no reason to feel terrible or depressed about your looks. And the good news is that there's more than one way to be attractive. Yes, typically, when we think of attractiveness and how people perceive it, it has a lot to do with bodily symmetry, having clear skin, and even the shape of your face. The fewer "imperfections" someone has, the more beautiful they are perceived to be. Weight and shape of the body certainly play a factor. Years ago, men would speak of child-bearing hips as something they desired. Now some admire a booty so high you can set books on it. For some people, even skin and hair color play a role. But it's all subjective and changes not only by culture but even by era, as well as personal preference.

But if you're not attractive by those standards, it's not all bad news. You'll find the key to beauty in the next chapter.

What if your issue goes deeper than skin deep?

We've been talking a lot about how to come to terms with your outer shell and about knowing your worth and loving yourself right where you're at. However, you may be suffering from something that goes much deeper than the surface area we've been talking about. Before you move on, I want to check in with you. You picked up this book hoping that by the end of it, you'd be a different person—someone who makes better choices; someone who could live with yourself, have more confidence, and perhaps figure out how the rest of your life can be the best of your life. Well, the truth is, any book can change your life, if you do the work. But you may have specific issues that have stunted you, paralyzed you, or held you back from moving ahead, and you may not even know what they are or how to deal with them. Does that sound like you?

To be able to move on and get to a better place, you're going to have to dig a little deeper than you've gone before. Perhaps you'll have to face things you've not wanted to look at, dig up and address some things you've had buried, so you can peel back the layers and find the true source of your pain and unhappiness. After I finished writing *You Are Worthy,* I realized people were uncovering more and deeper issues. There was underlying pain from their past keeping them from embracing their worth, and that's why I created a separate program—to help you dig deeper and remove those unwanted thorns that have been hurting you for years:

ADDITIONAL RESOURCE

Because of people just like you, I've created a mini-course called "The DIVINE Solution" to help you finally get to the root cause of the overwhelm and pain in your life.

This is the solution you've been looking for to:

- heal your soul
- dry your tears
- decrease tension and anxiety

...and finally be able to breathe again.

I'll guide you through my 6-step method to find and fix whatever is causing you to feel pain about yourself or your past.

WARNING: There will be some soul-searching on your part!

This program is designed to uncover wounds that have been holding you back from your total healing. In the same way that a doctor must sometimes re-break a bone to set it properly so it can finally heal, this searching inside yourself, evaluating, and asking questions may be uncomfortable for a time as you uncover things you can no longer ignore. But as with the reset bone, finding that you don't have to "limp" through life anymore is liberating, and the effort is always worth it.

The DIVINE Solution will help you find and fix whatever is causing you heartache related to your view of yourself, so you can leave your painful past behind, discover the right solution for you, and live the rest of your life with joy and belief that the big, beautiful future you've only dreamed about is available to YOU!

This mini-course is *valued at $497,* but because you picked up this book, it's **yours for only $39.** Get "The DIVINE Solution" by going to KatherineNorland.com/Divine.

Chapter Eight

How to Be Irresistibly Beautiful

What is the single most important and powerful trait you can possess to look more attractive? Confidence. And it's attainable. For everyone. Did you know that people who are confident are perceived to be more attractive?

If you do the inner work of discovering your value, learning to love yourself, and becoming who you were meant to be, you'll not only have the confidence to go after your dreams, but you'll also care less about what others think of you. That confidence will, in turn, have people perceive you as more attractive whether anything outwardly has changed or not.

> *"No matter how plain a woman may be, if truth and honesty are written across her face, she will be beautiful."*
>
> *— Eleanor Roosevelt*

If you're kind, you're attractive; if you tell the truth, it makes you very attractive. It demonstrates confidence in yourself.

If you perceive yourself to be beautiful and you're confident in your own skin, you behave differently. And when you behave in a more self-assured way, you come across to others as someone much more attractive. Think of the different kinds of body language you see in someone who doubts themselves versus someone who thinks they're capable of anything they put their mind to.

(In Lesson One of my online course "You Are Worthy," I cover why your posture and body language are important in order to build your confidence. In that lesson, you'll not only discover what your body language communicates, but also how you can use it to your advantage, because of how it's been scientifically proven to change both your psychology and your hormones. To find out more, go to KatherineNorland.com/Worthy.)

During the time in my life when I wouldn't leave the house without makeup on, I wasn't confident in who I was, just the way God made me. I am now. I don't have to spend all that time doing my hair and makeup each day. I'm confident to go out in public and speak my mind even to people who may be of a higher social status than I. I don't think anyone thinks I'm ugly anymore, even when I don't have makeup on (and even if they do, I don't care).

Every temporary fix we come up with stops working sooner or later. By the end of this book, you'll learn how to have the true confidence you need to accomplish your goals in life, just the way you are, without having to rely on any fake sense of security, cologne, wardrobe, surgery, college degrees, or anything else. When you see yourself differently, it causes you to act and respond differently.

Research has shown that people who think of themselves as attractive have actually been found to be more confident. It can go either way: Think of yourself as attractive and you'll be confident; or be confident, and people will think you're attractive.

How does that help you?

Confident people are perceived as more charming, and research has found that they also have more chance of finding their dream job and earning more money. You can do that through confidence, not just through a rockin' body and the perfect dye job. There's a chapter coming up to help you see yourself differently, which changes everything for the better.

When you are unafraid to be you, comfortable in your skin, and at peace with who you are, it shows. Your confidence radiates, and people treat you differently. Throughout this book, I've been talking about seeing yourself and loving yourself the way God does, and you can do that by getting to know His word and what He thinks of you. You can also do that by getting to know yourself. That involves peeling back the layers of who you are, what's important to you, and what moves your heart and fills you with purpose. Also, it will reveal that there's much more to you than meets the eye. When you get to know yourself, you'll realize that you're a pretty incredible creation made by God's design. You were born to do something noteworthy with your life, and nothing about your exterior needs to change for that to happen. Some of the most powerful and confident people in history haven't been all that pleasing to the eye and would never end up on the cover of a fashion magazine.

We must embrace the fact that God made each of us to be unique, like a beautiful floral arrangement. There are millions of different kinds of flowers, and you would be hard-pressed to find an ugly flower. I looked up "ugly flowers" on the Internet, and even the ones some considered ugly had their own special allure, whether it was their color scheme, shape, texture, or fragrance. It can be the same with us. Many of us feel that as we get older we lose our appeal, and we aren't as spectacular anymore. But I'd argue that a flower is not at its best when it's young, a tightly closed fresh bud. It's at its best when it's had time to live a little, open itself up fully to the world, and be in full bloom. Like flowers, only when we come out of hiding who we are, live a little, and open ourselves up to the world in full bloom, can people truly appreciate our splendor.

What God thinks is beautiful

Are you wondering what God's take is on all this? Do you think God prefers us to be plain and dowdy? He was in charge of our genetics and how we turned out. He obviously doesn't mind if people are beautiful, since He made them that way. We know He loves beauty just by looking around us at the flowers, the sea, and the sunsets. And God thinks you're magnificent. "You are altogether beautiful, my darling; there is no flaw in you" (Song of Solomon 4:7 NIV).

The last chapter was all about the pursuit of hotness and why it seems important. I vacillated for years between "hotness" and "holiness," pursuing one to the detriment of the other. There are obviously a lot of plus sides to both, but honestly, if I were to ask you what images come into your mind when you think of a holy person, do you think of a Rabbi who's a hundred years old? Mother Theresa? Gandhi? Or God himself? Or do you think of people who are so far removed from the world and the current reality we live in that there's no way they would understand our modern age or be able to blend in and make friends?

Do you think that if you pursued holiness, it would mean you could never go to the movies, dance, or cut your hair? Do you think you have to go to church every time the door is open, be stoic and boring, and never laugh? Or that it would mean you'd only wear baggy frocks from head to toe that show no skin and make your shape look like Mrs. Potato Head?

Perhaps you have an aversion to wanting to be holy because it seems absolutely unattainable, or you're someone who's had bad experiences with religious people who thought they were more holy than you and pointed out all the reasons God wasn't pleased with you for your behavior? I mean, who'd want to be judgmental and out of touch with society, like those finding fault with everyone but themselves?

Should we be holy or hot? Did you know it's actually possible to be both? They're not mutually exclusive. One of my favorite evangelists, Cheryl Salem, was actually Miss America 1980. In the same way that it's easy to misconceive what holiness looks like, "being hot" does not require you to starve yourself to resemble a lollipop stick with a bobbing head or wear an entire makeup counter on your face while wearing less cotton on your body than a Q-Tip. Beauty starts on the inside and makes its way out. A godly woman radiates in a way no high-end bronzing cream or even the Hope Diamond can.

Once you've got a handle on fixing your inside rather than worrying about your outside, only then would I even suggest some sort of makeover. I'm at a place now where I don't question whether it's better to be holy than hot. If I've only got half an hour to spare in my day, should I exercise or read the word? Paul answers that for us: "For physical training is of some value, but godliness has value for all things, holding promise for both the present life and the life to come" (1 Timothy 4:8 NIV). While there's nothing wrong with looking good, the pursuit of hotness needs to be replaced with our pursuit of holiness. That's where you must put your time, focus, and energy. God time for my spirit beats anything I could do for my outer shell (though sometimes I do both and go on a prayer walk). I'd rather be the ugliest person in Heaven than the sexiest person in Hell. In my upcoming book "You Are Loved," you'll find out exactly how much God loves you and how pleasing Him—getting His approval—is not as distressing as you may think.

In the last chapter, I mentioned some benefits of being hot. Are you wondering if there are benefits to being holy? Honestly, there are enough to fill a book of its own. I'll cover just three of those benefits.

1. It brings you closer to God. "Blessed are the pure in heart, for they shall see God" (Matthew 5:8 ESV). "LORD, who may dwell in your sacred tent? Who may live on your holy mountain? The one whose walk is blameless…" (Psalm 15:1-2 NIV).

Those who do their best to live a holy and blameless life get access to places no one else can go—sacred places where blessings abound.

2. It allows us to have a special assignment from God. I love this one. For those of you who feel common and believe there's nothing special about you, listen to this verse: "In a large house there are articles not only of gold and silver, but also of wood and clay; some are for special purposes and some for common use" (2 Timothy 2:20 NIV).

That's kind of like us ... do you ever feel that way? You look at someone and think, *Man, they're really special, they've got charisma, they're smart, talented, a great speaker, they have a wonderful family, they're powerful, or come from a better background ... they're gold and silver, they're made for special purposes; and me, I'm just wood and clay. I'm just here for common use, nothing special.* If you've ever felt that way, listen to the next verse. "Those who cleanse themselves from the latter [common or dishonorable things, depending on the translation] will be instruments for special purposes, made holy, useful to the Master and prepared to do any good work" (2 Timothy 2:21 NIV).

Do you hear that? If you cleanse yourself, if you strive to live holy, not only will you be close to God, but you'll also be used for special purposes and prepared for every good work. It's not your background, your status, your family, or where you grew up, if you grew up on the wrong side of the tracks or in the caste system or other rigid social groups that decide how far you can go or what you can achieve. It doesn't matter if no one recognized your worth. It doesn't even matter if your former actions made you a dishonorable vessel by God's standards. If you cleanse yourself, you'll have a special purpose and be prepared for every good work. The kind of preparation the Lord is looking for has nothing to do with you getting the best internships, being groomed for success by some powerful person, or being mentored by millionaires and given a boost up. God will set you up in a way no human can.

3. It causes those who don't love God to turn to Him. You, by living holy, can do that. No amount of arguing, debating, trying to tell people about God or why you're right about the scriptures, or even witnessing to them, can do that. It's the discernible, undeniable witness before them of your good, holy living in action that compels them to turn to Him.

Check this out. This is who you are and what you're capable of:

"But you are God's chosen treasure—priests who are kings, a spiritual 'nation' set apart as God's devoted ones. He called you out of darkness to experience his marvelous light, and now he claims you as his very own. He did this so that you would broadcast his glorious wonders throughout the world" (1 Peter 2:9 TPT).

"For at one time you were not God's people, but now you are. At one time you knew nothing of God's mercy, because you hadn't received it yet, but now you are drenched with it! My divinely loved friends, since you are resident aliens and foreigners in this world, I appeal to you to divorce yourselves from the evil desires that wage war within you" (1 Peter 2:10-11 TPT).

"Live honorable lives as you mix with unbelievers," (oh goodness, get ready for this next part), "even though they accuse you of being evildoers." Has that happened to you—someone accusing you of something so heinous that someone had to help you pick your jaw up off the floor afterwards? It happened to me twice recently. I was completely shocked by what these people accused me of. (But here's where it gets really good.) When we live holy lives, scripture tells us, "For they will see your beautiful works and have a reason to glorify God in the day he visits us" (1 Peter 2:12 TPT).

Doesn't that just touch your heart? Friends, even unbelievers who want nothing to do with God will be compelled to change. Those who accuse you of living wickedly, when they see your behavior and beautiful works, will be moved enough to find it possible to glorify God because of you. You have the ability, by living holy, to save people's souls from an eternity in Hell.

Let me tell you, no amount of steroids for beefing up, or Botox for smoothing out, can change you and the world around you and make you feel as good as living holy can.

If you're being honest, would you say you spend more time worrying about how you look to others than about whether you're pleasing God and looking good by His standards? Have you spent more time, money, and effort on your appearance than on helping others or doing charitable deeds? I'm not finger-pointing. I only want you to ask yourself this to get a gauge for where you've been and give you a little guidance and clarity.

Is there a better way?

Let's hear what Peter has to say about how it's possible to be irresistibly beautiful:

"Do not let your adornment be merely outward—arranging the hair, wearing gold, or putting on fine apparel—rather let it be the hidden person of the heart, with the incorruptible beauty of a gentle and quiet spirit, which is very precious in the sight of God" (1 Pet 3:3-4 NKJV).

In the New King James Version, it says not to let our adornment be *merely* outward (as in not *only* outwardly). The NIV says your beauty should not come from outward adornment; in other words, the main way you should be beautiful is through who you are on the inside.

Here's the verse in The Passion Translation: "Let your true beauty come from your inner personality, not a focus on the external. For lasting beauty comes from a gentle and peaceful spirit, which is precious in God's sight and is much more important than the outward adornment of elaborate hair, jewelry, and fine clothes" (1 Pet 3:3-4 TPT). It's saying our inner personality is much more important than outer beauty.

A friend and mentor of mine who is no longer with us, Tim Oman, was telling me about his time in New York when he was directing the play *Romeo and Juliet*. The theater company told him he could cast whomever he wanted for the roles, except for Juliet; she was already cast. And he was thinking, "Well, this woman better be something spectacular both in looks and ability," because Juliet, by his assumption, was the most romantic character ever devised. She was womanhood in flower, someone ready to be ravished. And when he saw the woman, he said she was a toad. He scratched his head, trying to figure out why on Earth this woman would have gotten the role of Juliet. But when he saw her perform the role, all the outward stuff faded into the background and her essence—who she was in her totality—struck such a chord in Tim that he said, "The most beautiful movie star in the world couldn't hold a candle to how breathtaking this woman was in her performance." And that was something no one with better aesthetics could touch.

What is interesting in the definition of personality is that it's "the visible aspect of one's character." No matter the kind of character you have, your personality is what makes that visible and impressed on others. To "impress" is to affect someone's mind or feelings deeply or strongly, or to influence their opinion, or to fix something in someone's mind or memory. When The Passion Translation says to let your beauty come from your inner personality, we can tell if you've been working on your inner man or your inner personality rather than the external. Your personality is actually what shows the outside world the content of your character, who you are, and what's inside you. These are clear by what you do and how your character is, and the impression it leaves on people.

The psychological definition of personality is *the sum total of the physical, mental, emotional, and social characteristics of an individual.*

If someone claims they're working on their inner person, and changing their heart, it would be apparent by how they behave and what kind of character they display in their personality. If nothing changes in their character and behavior, whatever they're doing with their inner person isn't working.

Back to the verse in 1 Peter: in The Message version, it says, "What matters is not your outer appearance—the styling of your hair, the jewelry you wear, the cut of your clothes—but your inner disposition. Cultivate inner beauty, the gentle, gracious kind that God delights in" (vv. 3:3-4 MSG).

> Disposition: *"The predominant or prevailing tendency of one's spirits; natural mental and emotional outlook or mood; characteristic attitude."*

Let me paraphrase what they're talking about in this translation with an example: It's better to have a faith-filled, happy demeanor, even if you're wearing rags, than to be in the most expensive designer clothes and be grumpy and pessimistic. The verse is saying outer beauty is not what matters. It's not totally forbidden to fix yourself up. God isn't concerned if you wax your legs or pluck your unibrow; He just wants your main focus to be on your inner person, not your outer appearance.

Let's look at one last version. The New Living Translation says, "Don't be concerned about the outward beauty of fancy hairstyles, expensive jewelry, or beautiful clothes. You should clothe yourselves instead with the beauty that comes from within, the unfading beauty of a gentle and quiet spirit, which is so precious to God" (1 Peter 3:3-4).

"If I have lived my call, exchanged my life for His, it's immaterial what size my casket is."

These verses aren't here to tell us we have to look like a total mess and never comb our hair or take a shower because it's only the heart that matters. I mean, how are you going to draw people to the splendor, beauty, and glory of God if they need a gas mask to sit next to you? Remember, we represent the King of kings, so it's okay to look nice or to have a pleasing appearance, as long as it's not consuming you, taking up all of your time, money and thought life.

To be irresistibly beautiful, you must allow your inner beauty to trump your outer beauty. God won't measure your waistline or make you step on a scale to determine if you get to go to Heaven (unlike some TV shows I've auditioned for!). As I wrote in my book *Poetic Prescriptions for Eternal Youth,* if I have lived my call, exchanged my life for His, it's immaterial what size my casket is.

If you're still thinking about putting your bod from God on the chopping block and going through with a cosmetic surgery, talk to God about it before you talk to your friends. Get His opinion before theirs. He loves being involved in every decision that we make. "Cast all your cares on Him, because He cares for you" (1 Pet 5:7).

What really matters

Here are some things I'd like you to consider. It doesn't matter if you're pro or con on the plastic surgery debate. It doesn't matter that your virgin hair has never been colored. It doesn't even matter that simply for beauty's sake, you've been poked more than a pin cushion. What matters is your heart. Is your heart striving after what's pleasing to God? What will matter is how you lived your life.

Did you follow your heart and your purpose? Did you live life to the fullest? Did you appreciate the body God gave you? Did you sacrifice your time in service to others? If the only thing people remember about you is that you had "work done" or looked great in a pair of jeans, then you won't have made the contribution to this world that needed to be made, that no one else was capable of making but you.

Let's keep the focus off ourselves and our flaws, and let's believe God, who tells us we're worthy just the way we are. Let's get out of our own way, and get busy finding ways to serve the world, which is in desperate need of help. Let's stop asking, "Am I good enough?" But rather, let's ask: "How can I use my gifts, talents, money, ideas, compassion, and maybe even my looks, with however much I currently have of them, to aid a fallen world and point the people in it to the God who not only loves them and can improve their earthly lives, but can also save them for eternity?"

> *"This is the true joy in life, the being used for a purpose recognized by yourself as a mighty one..."*
> *— George Bernard Shaw*

How do we do that? You may be thinking, "I'd love to get the focus off myself, but I've got too many things wrong with me. I want to serve God better and live my calling and purpose, whatever that is, but look at me; who would listen to me?" If you feel like that in the slightest, the next couple of chapters will smash that way of thinking. You'll be able to separate who you are from the body you live in.

Chapter Nine

How You Look Is Not as Important as How You See Yourself

Have you considered that what you think is your problem may go much deeper than skin deep? But how exactly do you get past what you don't like on the outside to find the real you? And how do you separate the person you see staring back in the mirror, that you think is you, from the unseen spirit you can't see but is really you? How do you grasp that the real you isn't the body you live in?

For me, even though I'd gotten to the place where I knew my outside didn't matter to God, and He'd love me regardless of whether my earth suit was shaped like a toothpick or Mount Kilimanjaro, I still hadn't come to love myself yet for how I appeared on the outside. I was caught up in the things of the world and not immersed enough in God's truth. Jesus told us in the book of Luke, "Look at the lilies and how they grow. They don't work or make their clothing, yet Solomon in all his glory was not dressed as beautifully as they are. And if God cares so wonderfully for flowers that are here today and thrown into the fire tomorrow, he will certainly care for you. Why do you have so little faith? And don't be concerned about what to eat and what to drink. Don't worry about such things. These things dominate the thoughts of unbelievers all over the world, but your Father already knows your needs" (Luke 12:27-30 NLT).

I worried about my body's exterior, thinking it was tied to

who I was. I loved God and wanted to live my life for Him but didn't know how to love myself because of the way I looked. Frankly, I didn't even think God wanted us to love ourselves. I used to think self-love was selfish or egotistical, and our lives should only be about Him and others (even if it was at our peril).

How did I start loving or even being at peace with the outer shell I was living in? It wasn't easy, especially considering that I live in Los Angeles, where the most beautiful people from all over the world move when they're told growing up, "You're utterly stunning, you should be an actress or a model." Plus, I was listening to the lies of the devil and the feedback from cold and callous casting directors, producers, and directors in the entertainment industry who, for the sake of giving honest feedback, let me know all the reasons they thought I wasn't right for the part outwardly. Never did it have to do with my heart and only rarely was it something other than my looks, like my voice. I didn't know how it was possible to separate who I was from the body I lived in when I was constantly ripped apart and judged by the outside. It made me feel like that's all there was to me.

A director put his hand on my shoulder after an audition and exclaimed, "Jeeze, you're like a linebacker!" Another grabbed my bingo wing and shook it, saying, "What is this, what is this?" Another backhanded me in the stomach and said, "Lose this, or you're not going to fit into the costume," and yet another criticized me when he took another actress and me to breakfast, and I ordered a whole bacon, egg, hash brown, toast, and orange juice meal while my skinny and perfect cohost ordered only grapefruit and coffee. Hey, I'm going to take advantage when I'm getting a free breakfast!

Later that same director of a TV show I was hosting grabbed and squeezed my squishy love handles and told me "You're too fat, you're fired." I wondered if I would've had such low self-esteem or would have gotten over it quicker if I'd chosen to be a librarian rather than an actress. Yet, in all honesty, I even hated myself in high school and loathed myself when I was a waitress, a factory worker, a dry cleaner, and a valet. Being in front of cameras isn't what started the self-hate; it just added more pressure to look perfect. The disgust I had for myself was already there.

I learned that God saw me as very good and more breathtaking than the sunset. He made me in His image, on purpose for a purpose; I knew that when He looked at me, He wasn't judging my outer package. His beauty contest had to do with the intent of my heart, but I was stuck in this reality where I was booking acting jobs or not booking them based on my outer shell, which I felt was the only thing that mattered to the rest of the world. I allowed the negative feedback from others to be my focus rather than God's thoughts towards me. I let their voices be louder than His. I meditated on what they said about me more than I did what the word of God had to say. I eventually learned how God felt, yet even after I knew what the scriptures said about me, it didn't automatically make me accept or love myself. But changing my outlook did.

Changing Your Outlook

I was in bondage to what's called a body dysmorphic disorder, i.e., a distorted body image and obsessions about *perceived* physical shortcomings. These flaws weren't even necessarily there or as bad as I saw them. Even when I was a teenager, without a wrinkle or gray hair and more fit and toned, I could find dozens of flaws in my appearance. This view of myself made me unhappy and unable to venture out of my shell or even think I could go after my dreams. I was constantly sabotaging myself. Sabotaging is what people do when they are at war with other people or countries. But I was at war with myself.

In order to start loving yourself right now for all that you are and all that you're not, you're going to have to change your outlook. When I changed my outlook, it changed everything. Your outlook is your point of view; your mental attitude; how you see the future. Here's the wonderful thing about changing it: I learned that when you change your outlook, you don't have to change your outward looks.

> ***When you change your outlook, you don't have to change your outward looks.***

Let me share with you how I did that. You may think you'd be more confident if you looked better, but haven't you also seen evidence in others to the contrary? Have you known people or seen some on TV who prove it's not about what your earth suit looks like, but how you feel about yourself despite what your outer shell looks like? You can probably attest to flipping through TV channels and stumbling upon rambunctious people on talk shows like Jerry Springer. You see these folks wearing as few clothes as a lingerie model even though they look like Jabba the Hutt, and they are out there on stage doing what I call the "tabloid TV strut," thinking they're hot and you're not, and they're in your face giving it all they've got. They're arguing with the audience about how everybody wants them. As they are getting booed, they're tossing their hair around and with big grins on their face saying, "You're just jealous." And they mean it. They love themselves ... a little too much. Even so, when people told them they were too big, and they needed to lose weight, or they needed to fix something about their looks, they didn't buy into it or let it affect how they saw or carried themselves. And you don't need to buy into the lie that your body isn't good enough either.

At the opposite end of the spectrum, thinking of my two friends who actually do look like lingerie models, I came to find out that they weren't even happy. Though they looked like goddesses, they didn't love themselves. They suffered from the same self-worth issues I had. Getting gobs of work done or starving themselves to be size 00 didn't fill up the empty spaces in them. And when I didn't love myself for the unique creation God made me, they were the very type of people I'd have compared myself to, wishing I looked like them so that I could be happy. My gorgeous friends were miserable and weren't going to have joy or be satisfied with themselves because they weren't viewing themselves the way God viewed them, but rather by the things this fallen world judges us by. I used to do the exact same thing.

When I finally got over myself, I still had the acne and was starting to see age spots on my face, and random hairs grew out of my chin. I started to love myself and be confident in who I was, despite what my earth suit looked like.

When I found love for myself no matter what I looked like and was at least 30 pounds heavier than the standard actress in Hollywood, I was offered a role in a film. The director said, "You're going to have to lose 20 pounds to do the role." I found loving myself just the way I was made me more self-assured, and came with a new boldness. The old me would have freaked out, had anxiety, and tortured myself in a crazy cycle of trying to diet and then binging on junk food because I was calorie-deprived. I would have spiralled down into depression, hating myself for the curves and my big bone structure. I'd have been in torment.

Instead, here are some things I did differently that helped change my outlook. If you do them, it'll help change yours as well.

1. ***Focus on your positive traits.*** The wonderful thing about focusing on your positive traits is that it helps you be at peace with your outer package and yourself as a whole, because your eyes are on what's good about you and not on what isn't. It even affects your way of being and operating in the world. I'd have never stood up to a director if I didn't have belief in myself like I do now. And it's not really belief in myself, but in who God made me to be.

2. Even more importantly, ***focus on what God says about you and how He sees you***. It wasn't about how this director saw me. It was about how God saw me. Knowing who I was in

Christ and how He saw me, I was finally at a place where I didn't panic when the director asked me to lose weight.

Rather than react in my old way, I calmly read the script to see if it was a legitimate request. I didn't see anything in the script that would say there was a weight requirement. I wasn't going to be playing someone with an eating disorder, or someone starved in prison, or anything like that. God had made me confident in who I was, so now I knew I didn't have to grovel to get work. And without any fear of what he would think, or worry about my career and losing the part, I was able to tell the director, "No, thank you. If you want someone 20 pounds lighter, then hire someone who is 20 pounds lighter." The first few times I stood up for myself like that, even I couldn't believe it. I wasn't going to listen to others' opinions, even if it meant I might lose a job or two, because I knew that "*what God had for me was for me and me alone, no one could take from me, not even Barbie's clone*" (excerpt from my *Poetic Prescriptions for Eternal Youth* book).

In the line of business I'm in, as an actress in the entertainment industry, we're often treated like products, not people. It was very hurtful during the first 10 or 15 years I pursued this career. I'd see women who were less talented actresses get the role because of how much better they looked.

Yet when I changed my outlook, a key benefit was that *I was able to change my view on rejection and be okay with it*. I began to know it wasn't a personal attack when they said no, nor did it change my value as a person.

The next benefit was that *I was able to stop connecting who I am to the shell I live in*. My getting told at auditions, "You're too short, tall, fat, pale, young, old," etc., no longer became an issue of my worth. My spirit is who I really am (which you'll learn more about in the next chapter). It's who God made before He put me in this temporary housing unit. My spirit has far more value and will live for eternity after my body dies and I leap out of this tent. When they rejected me because my outer package wasn't what they were looking for, it became okay with me. They wanted a two-story house or a castle, maybe a tiny home, or one with a tan or brown exterior, and that's not what I'm living in. My housing unit just wasn't right for that job. And when there was a job calling for a white, double-wide trailer, I'd get my shot!

When you get to this place of acceptance, if you are ever rejected by a friend, a potential mate, or anyone else because of how you look, you just let it go. You realize that God loves you and wants you to succeed, and it's not over for you. If someone can't see your value because of something as insignificant as the shape of the dust bag you're living in, it's their loss, not yours. You must know God is lining up the right people to come into your life who'll love you and cherish you just the way you are, with all your cracks and faults, interior and exterior.

Are you wondering how on Earth I changed my outlook? I mentioned that the second thing I did was to focus on how God saw me. You know, when we get older, our faces start to sink in and droop down and have some cracks, and to take care of it in the physical, we would go to a cosmetic surgeon or a medi-spa and get dermal fillers to plump it up. These injectable fillers are gel-like substances injected beneath the skin to restore lost volume, smooth lines and soften creases, or enhance facial contours. Well, in the same way, my soul had gotten worn down and started to sink in and look hollow because of all I'd been through in life and the attacks of the enemy. I had to make several visits to see the God-medic surgeon. I had to go to God and get some soul filler, lots of it. It's still something I have to do on a regular basis. When my focus changed to how God sees me, it buffed out all of the cracks and perceived shortcomings.

Knowing who God says you are

3. ***Get filled up with God's word.*** I want to show you the effect on me when God's word became my filler, rather than collagen. Filling up with God's word is the most important thing you can do to change your outlook about yourself. When I finally did, what He said about me filled in all my cracks. When I was plump with the word, each crevice and hollow in me was gone. I finally knew God loved me, and all I needed to do in return was humbly trust and obey Him, and He'd make everything work out for me. He'd answer my prayers and give me a more abundant life.

Then, I came to a huge realization of what had been holding me back, and when I figured it out, I was never the same. Here it is: God didn't have a problem with who I was; I had a problem with who I *thought* I was because I didn't know who God *said* I was. You've got to get this: The reason you feel you don't fit in is that you don't know who you are. *You will never truly know WHO you are until you know WHOSE you are.*

You must believe you are God's precious child, made in His image and likeness; and with Him nothing will be impossible for you (Luke 1:37). Nothing can stop you, and nothing can separate you from God's love. Nothing about who you are, what you look like, mistakes you've made, or any other flaw you believe holds you back, has any power to override the magnificent plans God has for your life—unless you let it.

> ***You will never truly know WHO you are until you know WHOSE you are***

To know who you are, you've got to load your plate with the word of God like you're sitting down at the buffet, feasting on His holy word like fried chicken, until your spirit man is big enough to pop all the buttons off your little religious shirt and you're bigger than the incredible hulk in the spirit realm! When you do, any challenge you're faced with will be no match for you. Pumping iron at the gym helps a tiny bit with strength, but gorging on God's word will make you strong in more ways than can be measured. All areas of your life benefit when you focus on the word: God's word is profitable for ALL things (2 Timothy 3:16). There is nothing in your life it won't help.

I was wimpy and atrophied in the spirit realm, which is why I couldn't accomplish the desires in my heart. The strength I needed had to come from His Spirit to my innermost being. Paul tells the Ephesians, "I pray that out of his glorious riches he may strengthen you with power through his Spirit in your inner being, so that Christ may dwell in your hearts through faith. And I pray that you, being rooted and established in love, may have power, together with all the Lord's holy people, to grasp how wide and long and high and deep is the love of Christ…" (Ephesians 3:16-18 NIV).

God doesn't have a problem with who you are; you have a problem with who you THINK you are because you don't know who God SAYS you are.

4. ***Root yourself in His word.*** My confidence was weak, and my faith was puny, because I wasn't rooted, grounded and established in His love. Instead, I was rooted and grounded in my inability and what I thought were flaws. I was stuck in anxiety, petrified by my fears, and unable to move. My whole life was operating from a place of fear. Have you ever felt that way, afraid to try something because you might fail? Afraid to speak up for yourself because you don't want confrontation? Afraid to raise your hand because your answer might be wrong? Afraid to do something in your heart because people might judge you? John tells us, "There is no fear in love; but perfect love casts out fear, because fear involves torment. But he who fears has not been made perfect in love" (1 John 4:18 NKJV). Scripture tells us God is love (1 John 4:8). If we are in God, we should have no fear, but should be absolutely full of faith. The key benefit of rooting yourself in His love is, *you'll drop the fear and pick up faith.*

What I'm about to say may sound a little harsh, but it's important for you to grasp. You will never reach your goals UNLESS you can back them up with the FAITH needed to make them happen. Hebrews 11:1 in the NIV tells us, "Now faith is confidence in what we hope for and assurance about what we do not see." Here the word is confidence (the way I'm confident I know how to put my contact lenses in). The English Standard Version says faith is assurance (like being sure and positive the sky is blue), and the King James Version says it's substance. What is substance? It's tangible matter or material; it's a real concrete thing (the way I have a white SUV).

5. *Build your faith.* Our faith brings what we want and hope for from the supernatural realm into the natural realm. Our faith makes what we've prayed for manifest to the point where we can get our hands on it. It takes us from "God, I'm believing for this new job" to sitting at our desk at our new workplace.

Seeing yourself the way God does

Now you might ask, what does our faith level have to do with our outlook and our outward looks? I had to see myself as worthy, loved, chosen, capable, unstoppable, and victorious. Changing my outlook to the view God had of me allowed His point of view to hold more weight than any way I could see myself. I had to see past my looks, and when I did, I was able to perceive myself the way God saw me: as fully capable of achieving my dreams, just the way I am. When I did, it seemed like anything was possible for me, which was a great boost to my faith.

Have you ever seen one of those pieces of art that looks like one thing at first glance, but then someone tells you to look harder, and you stare at it longer, then suddenly a different picture emerges? The second picture overtakes you in such a way that you have a hard time going back and even seeing the other picture you saw first. You know you saw what you saw, but looking longer revealed something else you didn't know was there and wasn't visible at first glance.

That's how it is when your faith grows; you're able to replace the vision of yourself, what you see at first glance, that you think is you, and soon your faith helps you look deeper and see a picture of yourself you never saw before. You finally see the hidden picture of how God sees you, and once you do, you have a hard time going back to seeing the other picture. James tells us, "But he who looks into the perfect law of liberty [that's God's word] and continues in it, and is not a forgetful hearer but a doer of the word, this one will be blessed in what he does" (James 1:25 NKJV). When it says, "he who looks," many versions say this means to look intently, or carefully; to peer; to fix your view; to gaze deeply. It's not just a quick glance; it's the idea of eagerness and concentration. God's word is something you must search out completely to see the real true picture of who you are.

My faith grew in who He said I was when I took the time to examine His word, and soon I had the faith to make the substance of my dreams my reality. When I started to believe the picture of me that He saw and that I could do all things, I started to be able to do all things. When I believed I would write this book for you, only then could it move from the supernatural idea God gave me down into the natural, as the physical thing you're reading.

When my outlook became more important than my outward looks and what I saw at first glance, the key benefit I got was that *I could move in the direction of my dreams.*

Once you see yourself the way God sees you, it changes everything, because how you look is not as important as how you see yourself.

The negative thoughts I had about my looks, abilities and worth—basically my doubts—stopped God from doing any mighty works in me and through me. Instead of having His life-giving word running through me, I had a constant mantra that I was not good enough, smart enough, thin enough, or pretty enough. Those thoughts that I was downright ugly and unworthy were ricocheting like bullets through my brain. I wasn't allowing God to work through me because I hadn't been able to separate who I was from the body I lived in, and until I did, life was miserable and depressing. But, once I made that separation, I found freedom. Everything felt lighter; my feelings stopped getting hurt when people made negative comments, and I found joy. Next, I'll tell you how I did it.

Chapter Ten

You Are Not the Dust Bucket You Live In

There are several things to do or keep in mind that will help you make the separation between who you are and the body you live in. First, *you've got to be convinced they're two separate things.* You're not the dust bucket, or vessel, you're residing in. Me neither. I'm not these outward things—the forehead that keeps growing because the hairline is receding, the skin that has brown spots, the crow's feet, or the jowls that are starting to look like a hound dog. And neither are you. Your outer shell is not you. And yes, you may not like that it's breaking down, falling apart, or growing horizontally instead of vertically.

Spending time dwelling on the things you don't like won't change them. When you do that, it takes your focus off what God wants you to be focused on, *your relationship with Him*—living your life in a way that honors Him, points to Him, and leads others to Him.

I have a sign hanging in my house that says, "*A clean house is a sign of a misspent life.*" In one way, it's kind of a warning to friends and acquaintances that yes, there'll be toys on the floor, there'll be dirty dishes in the sink, and our family pets are dust bunnies. At any moment, you may step on something one of the kids dropped. In another way, though, it's saying that my concern and time are spent centered on the eternal things: the calling God's given me and the messages I feel He wants me to put into the world.

No, it's not an excuse to let our homes look like an explosion happened; there shouldn't be science experiments that used to be food rotting in every corner. We should still be able to walk barefoot in the house without cringing or stepping on some sticky-ickies. But a sparkling house doesn't need to be your priority unless in some way it's tied to your vocation or calling.

On a day we're having company over or an acquaintance who hasn't moved to family status yet, I may pick up my house. But I won't spend all day chasing after the kids and putting each toy in the toy box the moment they are done playing with it. I'm not running to clean each dish the moment someone dirties it; I'm lucky if it happens by that evening. I'm not worried about what someone might think if they happen to stop by and the house doesn't look like a showroom. That's not worthy of the precious little time we have on Earth.

I no longer spend 30 minutes in front of the mirror each day doing my hair and makeup, just in case someone might stop by unannounced. I know that the way I keep my house and how I keep the shell I live in (though they can be seen and judged by others, and should have some semblance of order) aren't where eternal rewards are found. There are many times when I've intentionally ignored some bit of housework or getting a much-needed haircut because God spoke something to my spirit, and I was working on obeying what I felt He was telling me to do. When I started to make myself open to His promptings rather than a slave to others' opinions and my to-do list, that's when He began downloading words of wisdom to me. Now I had gotten out of my own way and was available to capture and share His wisdom with the people who needed it.

If you're thinking, *Sounds great, I'd love to get my focus off myself and onto the things of God more, but I just don't know how to stop thinking about my earth suit,* here's one way that helps me switch my focus. I start to imagine the bigger picture: what my legacy will be when I die. What will I leave behind or be remembered for? I start to think of the hurting people around me now who I could be of service to, who need my time, kind words, or donations. It puts my focus where it should be and keeps me centered. It reminds me I'm not the dust bucket I live in, and I can do things for others outside of myself that have nothing to do with the shape and size of my tent and whether it has a few wrinkles.

When people speak of the dead, they rarely ever talk about what they looked like; no one cares if you wore size 4 or kept a perfect house. People talk about the difference someone made, what they learned from them, the charities and organizations they began or supported, their inventions, the books they wrote, and the recipes they passed down. What's left behind has nothing to do with these temporary vessels, but everything to do with how we touched and left our mark on mankind.

You are not your body

Here's how I know we are not the dust buckets we live in. God tells us in Jeremiah 1:5 (ESV): "Before I formed you in the womb I knew you, and before you were born I consecrated you; I appointed you a prophet to the nations." Do you hear that?

God knew you before you were in your mother's womb. He. Knew. You. The real you, before He put you in your body and placed you in your mother's body. Your body is not you. It's just a house you live in while on Earth. It has nothing to do with the real you, which means there's no point in being down on yourself if you don't like the one you're in.

Galatians tells us, "But when he who had set me apart before I was born, and who called me by his grace..." (Galatians 1:15 ESV). See, God already set you apart before you were born. He knew you before you were a twinkle in your parents' eyes and knew you'd be worthy. He set you apart for His purpose prior to sticking you in whatever body you have. He knew you'd make a difference regardless of the habitation you were in on Earth.

You and I are not these bodies of flesh and bones having a spiritual experience trying to get close to God. You and I are speaking spirits having a human experience who already came from God. We'll one day fly far from the constraints of this skin suit and live for all eternity, not just in the mansion God prepared for us, but in a body so glorious, nothing can compare to it. Besides being a good steward and giving this body the proper nutrients and occasional movement, I don't want to spend the little time I have on Earth trying to keep together what will eventually fall apart and come to nothing. Like a house becomes piles of rubble, my body will be food for worms. But that doesn't matter, because I won't be in it when the worms go to town on my carcass. The best use of my time here is to spend it with God and leading others to Him. Our physical house may get burned down; our physical bodies can't withstand the flames; but what we do for the kingdom is something tested in God's furnace that never gets burned up (1 Corinthians 3:13-15).

I recognize you may not be at that place yet where you feel like you can ignore or at least not put such emphasis on your temporary housing unit. You may be in the fitness profession or the clothing industry, and your outer package determines whether or not you put food on the table. I'm not talking about becoming a careless slob, letting everything go south to only focus on your spirit. I'm talking about not paying ridiculous amounts of attention to your outward casing. There's a healthy balance between despising how we look and putting zero effort into it, and being enamored with it, having what you eat and when you work out consume all your mental space. You don't need to freak out about missing a workout or having a single drop of oil on your food or the exact number of grams of protein you think you need. I'm talking about taking care of yourself like a good steward should, appreciating the body God gave you and using it to its full capacity to run the race He put you in to fulfill the mission He has you on Earth to do.

Although it doesn't matter what you look like on the outside, you do need to have a little bit of balance and not totally throw away taking care of yourself. I'm not saying that being a spirit is a license for you to not care at all or constantly indulge in all the finer things in life. Often, it's very beneficial to pull back and have the simplicity of eating like they did in the garden of Eden, enjoying all the fresh produce and natural things God made rather than laboratory-made scary Franken-foods in boxes, bags and cans. Not because your size matters, but because making healthier choices to be around for your family longer, and being on this earth disease-free long enough to carry out your God-given mission, is worth it. But even if you're not fit and healthy now, it's not acceptable to let your size keep you from finding joy in your daily life or going after your dreams.

The proper perspective

When I couldn't stand my own reflection, and my self-esteem was crushed like peanut shells at the corner bar, I was able to overcome this by seeing it from a different perspective. I found this new "view" by studying God's word and what He had to say about His workmanship.

Have you noticed that knowing what God's word has to say about you is a theme in this book? It should be the theme of every believer's life. Listen to what the book of James has to say about hearing the word of God but not doing it: "For if you listen to the word and don't obey, it is like glancing at your face in a mirror. You see yourself, walk away, and forget what you look like" (James 1:23-24 NLT). We can't be like that; we have to know the word and, in turn, know what we look like, and not in the natural realm. We must know what we look like to God in the supernatural. You may look in the mirror and see a lowly worm ready to be squished, but when God looks at you, He sees a powerful roaring lion made in His image. Once you know the word, you know God, and when you know God, you know who you are because you were created in His image and likeness. The following verses paraphrased from the Bible are the ones that helped me separate who I am from the dust bucket I live in.

"I am fearfully and wonderfully made" (Psalm 139:14); "My gray hair is a crown of glory" (Proverbs 16:31); "Man looks at the outward appearance, but God looks at the heart" (1 Samuel 16:7); "Beauty is fleeting, but a woman who fears the Lord should be praised" (Proverbs 31:30); "Beauty shouldn't come from outward adornment; the unfading beauty is a gentle and quiet spirit" (1 Peter 3:3-4); "We were created in God's own image" (Genesis 1:27); and, "God formed us from dust and breathed life into us" (Genesis 2:7). Yeah, see what I mean? We're just living in dust buckets. It's not the dust bucket, but the breath of life God breathed into it, that counts.

I could say something about each one of those scriptures, but for me, the one that really changed my perspective was 2 Corinthians 4:7 (KJV): "But we have this treasure in earthen vessels, that the excellency of the power may be of God, and not of us..."

Wait, what? We're not these dust buckets we live in? It's just a place where our treasure hides? Where we and the Holy Spirit reside? This verse lit up my brain like a million light bulbs. In my head I knew that when I died, my earthly body would be left here. I knew I'd get a new heavenly body someday. But for some reason, it hadn't occurred to me that if I was leaving my body behind, that IT wasn't ME. I'd thought I WAS this outer shell, and that belief was completely wrapped and tied with double fisherman's knots. If I tried to untie it or use force, it would only tighten more. I was convinced that if it looked better, I'd get more acting jobs, opportunities, and friends; I'd be able to attract a boyfriend or husband; I'd get more attention, love, and accolades; and my life would have meaning.

But when I really started to think about it, I realized that if my looks were improved, although it would make me feel better to receive the praises of others, it wasn't what I was created for. Living my life to get *recognition* about something that's aging faster than I'd want it to, decaying on levels I didn't even know about, all to have people WHO WILL NOT DETERMINE MY ETERNITY like me more, was a colossal WASTE of time—a maze I would never escape. I chased a hollow existence, going on diet after diet, beating myself up mentally or even punishing myself if I had one too many cookies. I wasn't enjoying life; I was suffering over silly things like how many pimples I had or the fact that I was wearing a size 14 when others wore size 4.

Maybe it's not perfect to be perfect

But the more I sought God, it became clear that those of us with the most cracks in our jars of clay, the ones who are the most broken down, can often be a better testament to the power and greatness of God, because God can shine through all those cracks. I discovered that people could see God even better in us when they're not distracted by perfect facial symmetry or the body of a Greek god or goddess, because with those features, people might think what we accomplish in life is due to our good looks, not the grace, favor and blessings of God.

People don't relate to perfect people. When you watch a movie, you're rooting for the underdog to win. You're relating to the character who's a mess and is trying to make something of their life. You're not relating to the guy or gal who owns a mansion, has perfect looks and multiple degrees from Ivy League colleges, has it all together, and has no flaws or problems.

When I let that thought sink in, I realized that having a perfect outside might actually work against me in sharing the gospel, because others wouldn't be able to relate to me or might only be listening for the wrong reasons. (Like the time I did prison ministry at the local jail, and the sheriff pulled me aside and asked me not to wear such short skirts, because some of the inmates were only coming to church to see me and not to listen to the gospel. But I digress.) Look at all the examples in the Bible of messed-up people who God used to make history. Not a single one of them was perfect. They all had flaws and were broken in some way. When I meditated on the truth of God's word, it gave me a check-up from the neck up. I got to a place where, when people put me down, I didn't crumble into a sloppy pile of pity tears. I found I was able to separate what they said about my exterior from who I was, the same way we know the house we live in isn't us. If I operate in His dominion, power, authority, signs, wonders, kindness, love, charity, and forgiveness, then I reflect who God is, no matter what I look like, and that attracts more people than you can imagine.

Who would you want to spend time with, work with, and hear about God from? Someone who has cracks and flaws outwardly, but behaves kindly, and loves and acts like God would? Or someone who looks like outward perfection but has an ego bigger than the universe and acts like the devil?

In the entertainment industry, if you're an actor or a model, you're considered a product, not a person. Before I was able to separate who I was from the dust bucket I lived in, it was soul-crushing to be judged. But since I've been able to separate myself from my earth suit, when I audition, I know I'll be judged on my outer package, and now I get it. I've learned to see from their perspective, and that I'll be assessed like a product (not the person I truly am).

From that view, if I'm a product—let's say a ketchup bottle—then I'd be an old-fashioned one, and I would have a vintage label on me and be made out of glass. Perhaps this role I'm auditioning for is a futuristic movie that requires the new fuller plastic ketchup bottles, with the lids upside down and an updated label. That doesn't mean the old label is bad. It only means it's not what they had in mind or is appropriate for this particular role. It didn't mean I was a terrible actor or a bad person, or nobody liked me, or I should quit doing what I love and move back to my hometown (not that I ever used to have those conversations with myself after every role I didn't get—okay fine, maybe I did, like, 600 times). But now, I finally get it. My exterior just wasn't what they needed for the role. We must be honest at some point about this outer shell and stop trying to make it something it's not. When my outer shell isn't what they had in mind for a role, it doesn't mean anything negative about the real me, the speaking spirit, this child of the living God having this earthly experience.

Being upset about how much or how little pigment our skin has, our height, our moles, freckles, or the length of our torso or shape of our ears does us no good, because those are things we have no control over. And if you can't do anything about it, why let it take up valuable real estate in your mind? As scripture says, if we're not able to do the little things, why be anxious about the rest? (Luke 12:26). Bashing my head against the wall because my eye colors don't match is no longer worth my valuable time.

This book isn't about whether fixing yourself up or not is okay. This is about finding out who you really are, accepting and loving yourself, knowing what God thinks about you, your true identity, and what's really important. After all, 100 years from now, is what you looked like going to matter? Or is your legacy going to be the thing you're remembered for? Let's make that the case. You've learned you're not the dust bucket you live in. You were around before you were put in your body, and God knew you. Now that you have the right perspective, we can talk about doing something to look a little better, or at least make the best of what you've got.

Chapter Eleven

Make the Best of What You've Got

When it comes to our talent or brains, the wonderful thing is that we can always improve upon them. We can acquire knowledge; we can practice developing our talent. But wishing it was some other way, that we were better or smarter, isn't going to change things. We've got to put some work into it. It's the same when it comes to our looks.

As we talk about this, it's important to keep what you've learned here in mind: 1) *Fixing the outside won't help an inside problem;* 2) *How you see yourself is more important than how you look;* and 3) *You're not the dust bucket you live in.* Now we can talk about doing something about our outside, because we're not obsessed with it anymore. We can talk about accentuating our positive traits. You can wear things that are flattering; you can style your hair, put a bit of concealer on undereye circles, clip on hair extensions, or even spray some hair on the balding spots. But for the most part, when it comes to you, what you see is what you get. It's an area unlike our brains or skills, which is not likely to get better as we age, but worse according to society's standards.

Of course, you have a choice: You can fight aging with all you've got and end up paying the mortgage on your plastic surgeon's third vacation home in Aruba, or you can choose to accept yourself and this natural aging process and say, "This is what I've got to work with, I'll just make the best of it." Hating the natural evolution and aging process isn't going to turn back the hands of time; it's only going to make you miserable. And if you're stressed out and angry about it, it's just going to give you more wrinkles.

Sometimes I see aging actresses around Hollywood or on their social media pages who were once considered to be the super-hot "flavor of the month." They were popular for their chiseled features, rocking bodies, and sometimes even their talent. But often, they've not developed themselves or their talent to the degree where they could stand on their own, without who they were being tied into their looks. And many times, they didn't take an interest in other ways to find fulfillment outside of their career, like hobbies, charities, or other things that give them joy.

They come across as if they're stuck in a time warp. Decades later, they're sporting their looks in the hair, makeup and outfits that got them noticed when they were in their 20s and 30s. And now they're in their 60s, desperately trying to cling to the version of sexy they used to be. And it looks wrong to smoosh all of their now "slightly floppier due to loss of elasticity" parts into the skin-tight mini-dress they wore 35 years ago. Even if it still fits, that doesn't mean they should wear it. This goes for men, too. Are you still trying to pull off your muscle shirts and thick gold chains with a dad bod, sunken chest, and ever-shrinking biceps? You might want to rethink that. I admit I'm not innocent of this either. I've done the same thing, squeezing into a tight pair of pants only to discover my once perky butt has now become a folded-over bag of floppy cottage cheese. I've needed to discover what works for me as my aging body goes from toned and tight to droopy. Thank you, gravity.

I'm not saying you can't be sexy or beautiful after a certain age, because there are multitudes of women and men who prove you can be at any age. Yet we must take an inventory at least every decade to discern whether or not what we're doing with our hair, makeup, and clothes is still serving us for where we're going and how we want to be perceived. As we age, things change and shift. This may be time for you to send half your wardrobe to the thrift store.

I'm not an expert in style or makeovers and won't be telling you all the tips and tricks to look good in each decade. There's tons of info on that online and plenty of books written if you want specifics on looking great at any age. But for now, when you get ready, just ask yourself these questions before you leave the house: Does wearing this or fixing myself up like this help me look and feel like I'm worthy and a child of the most-high God, which God says I am? Am I representing Him and His kingdom well in the way I'm choosing to present myself?

I recently did this. I'd tucked away several bins of clothes that were too small for me in my shed for over a decade, and after losing a bunch of weight from my last pregnancy, I pulled out all those tubs and tried on those clothes. I was excited many of them fit me again. But as I tried them on, I had a lot of short skirts that didn't seem short on me ten years ago. Apparently I've gotten thicker and the skirts needed to cover more mass, which made them not the length I remembered when I was a trimmer and more toned version of myself. Plus, my taste in clothes had shifted.

I found both skirts and tops that were either lower cut than I'd wear now or somehow tighter than before (I'm pretty sure they all just shrank sitting in those plastic tubs in the shed in the hot California sun, not because I've fluffed out; yeah, that's what I'm telling myself.) But either way, they didn't look proper on me anymore. Sure, I could squeeze into them. But should I? I mean, can you imagine me in a halter top and plaid schoolgirl skirt at my age? Don't answer that. I was able to fill up five jumbo bags of clothes to give away to my slimmer and more youthful friends who could pull off the look.

Though some of the clothes were still appropriate, they were a size smaller than what I wear now, and I had to make the decision: Am I really going to buckle down, give up bread, French fries, sugar, and my chocolate fix, and start doing high-intensity workouts? The answer was nope, not happening, not a chance. I have no problem adding more healthy food into my diet, as long as I still get my treats.

I don't care about being a certain size anymore. Not enough to obsess or be rigid about it. It doesn't bother me that you can't bounce a quarter off my abs but that it would just sink into the abyss of my gelatinous gut. Instead of having a couple of tubs of these clothes lying around that are labeled "too small," which could in the back of my head remind me every time I see them that I'm larger than I used to be, I got rid of them. *Sometimes clearing out the physical clutter also helps us clear the mental clutter* and come to terms with where we are at now.

Self-Improvement Is an Inside Job

This isn't to say there's no room for self-improvement; there always is. It just needs to be measured against the weightier matters of our calling and our purpose. Spending two hours a day at the gym would add up with drive time to at least three hours a day I could spend with my family, helping humanity, or working on my calling. That amount of time over what's left of my lifetime, since I plan to live to 121 in order to celebrate a 100-year wedding anniversary with my husband (although he doesn't seem to be on board with my plan to live that long, considering how much bacon he eats)—anyway, over the course of what's left of my lifetime, if I worked out that much, that would be over nine years spent doing the treadmill march in pursuit of a tight and toned earth suit. I could have spent that time writing a few more books, starting a business or charity, or finding other ways to make a change to help humanity.

Sometimes clearing out the physical clutter also helps us clear out the mental clutter

You just need to find that healthy balance, not underdo it or overdo it. Instead of spending nine years of the life I have left, if I work out at home for 30 minutes a day (which is what I'm striving for, I'm not there yet), I would have saved more than eight years I could use to do something that makes a lasting impact.

At some point, we have to get real with ourselves: We don't have the metabolism, collagen, or cell growth turnover we had 10, 20 or 30 years ago. But it doesn't mean you can't make the best of what you've got, or that you can't age gracefully. After all, scripture says, God

"...satisfies your mouth with good things, so that your youth is renewed like the eagle's" (Psalm 103:5 NKJV). Oh, and FYI, I just searched the web for natural foods to help you stay young, and avocados and dark chocolate are on the list. Whew. But seriously, the more time you spend with God, the better you look. We have a glow about us. I remember a period of time (before I had kids) when I'd been setting aside a couple of hours each morning for prayer, worship, seeking God, and letting Him pour out His wisdom and love on me. I knew it was changing me on the inside; I could feel it.

But it also started to make a difference on the outside. I was at an acting workshop, and I kept getting complimented on how I looked. I didn't wear anything out of the ordinary or do my hair and makeup any differently than normal, but my classmates saw me differently. One of my teachers, who did not believe in God, said, "Katherine, you're just glowing tonight." I knew what it was, and wanted to give God the credit, so I said, "That's the glory of God shining through me." Well, my acting teacher just laughed at me as if I were delusional. But I knew it was true.

Remember when Moses was on Mount Sinai and spent 40 days and nights with God getting the Ten Commandments? It made him glow. His face shone, and he wasn't aware that his face had become radiant from talking to the Lord. His people were taken aback by how he gleamed and were afraid to come near him. When Moses realized this, he started to wear a veil over his face when he talked to the people, which he'd remove when he spoke to the Lord (Exodus 34:29-35). This is one of the many benefits of spending time with the Lord. It doesn't only make us wiser and calmer; spending time with God is better than the most expensive laser skin resurfacing with diamond tips and 24-karat gold facial masks. The best self-improvement isn't an outside job, but an inside one.

Being busy with the right things

As an actor, I've had to come to terms with the ever-shifting roles I've been cast to play or not cast to play based on how I currently look or don't look anymore. When I started out, I'd play a lot of bad girls, the girls the guys would cheat with. Then I moved into playing "sweet wife" roles; then mom roles; and I'm sure it won't be long before I'm playing grandma roles. And yes, as I move along and graduate each decade, there do seem to be fewer roles I'm right for, but it's okay. I don't get upset about it, because there are lots of other things in life that make me happy, like coaching, teaching, writing, motivational speaking, and sharing with you the struggles I've gone through in hopes that it will help you find it a little easier to overcome yours. I'm not wrapped up in how much better I used to look. I'm making the most of what I've got now.

Sometimes, no matter how talented you are as an actor, if you just don't look the part of what they had in mind, you're not going to get the role, and it has nothing to do with your talent. In other lines of work, they usually look for the most qualified and won't put as much pressure on what the person looks like. The focus is on whether their skills are up to par, they're great with people, they know the technical aspects of the job, or they're a good sales closer.

I mentioned that actors are considered products, not people. I used to think it was pretty awful, until I realized that when producers or directors are putting shows together, they have to make sure the "products" tell the story at first glance, without words, because unless you're the star of the show, you don't have the whole movie, episode or season to enlighten people about who your character is. A casting person's concern, especially for the smaller roles, is that the audience knows right away that this guy is the skeezy, sleazy sales jerk, or this girl is the stereotypical ditzy dumb girl. Whether we book the role or not sometimes has nothing to do with talent or doing a good audition.

When you know you're not the shell you live in, you let rude comments or people's disapproval of how you look roll off your back, especially in the entertainment industry. But it applies to dating, too, because you know you're not going to be right for every part, or you're not going to be attractive to every potential suitor. There will be some parts for which you are right, and there will be people who like you and are attracted to you, where there is a spark or a connection. Just like the ketchup bottle analogy, you know the contents inside your bottle are just as good as someone else's. You could bring a lot of flavor to the role or the relationship and make that meal of words or dating experience much tastier if they'd give you a chance. But if you're not chosen, or someone doesn't "vibe" with you, that's okay. There will be other meals for you to flavor. Eventually, some will be hungry for and appreciate what you bring to the table.

When you're able to disconnect who you are from the body you live in, you don't take things so seriously. When you're not emotionally tied to how you look, you don't get upset if someone says you're too fat, too thin, or too wimpy; or you have a big nose, flat butt, or cankles, or whatever the remark is. It becomes irrelevant. And if there's nothing you can do about it anyway (other than take yourself to a chop shop), what's the point of dwelling on it? It does you no good, and you know from the last chapter that you are not the dust bucket you live in.

If someone insults you or puts you down, disregard it. Remember, we're supposed to be dwelling on the things that are noble, right, pure, lovely, of good report and praiseworthy (Philippians 4:8). If what someone said to you or thinks about you aren't those things, don't waste your time ruminating on it. Besides, what people say to you often says more about them than it does about you. Those people slinging mud on you are often not happy with themselves.

If we're busy running the race God told us to run, we won't be concerned about what anyone said to us. We'll be loving people, making a difference, and won't have time to be hurt or critical of anyone. When you're living your life focused on God's calling, you don't have time to point out flaws in others. You don't sit in a pit of hurt when someone's mean. You're focused on working out your own salvation (Philippians 2:12).

Buffing out insecurities and imperfections

It should feel insignificant to care if your body type doesn't allow you to wear the latest fashion. You've got the body you've got; you may as well make the most of it. Yet here's the thing: Even if you do look perfect on the outside, that alone doesn't assure you'll be at peace with yourself, or even like yourself, if you've got inner work to do. The hourglass look I once pined over won't make me happy if I haven't renewed my mind (which we'll talk about soon). If you've naturally got a look or a shape that others try hard to attain, good on you. I really hope you're happy, living out the call God gave you and running after your dreams. Yet I've seen too many times that having these perky perks doesn't guarantee you are.

Insecurity doesn't look good on anyone

I worked on a film with an actress who had a perfectly shaped body and who could have been on the cover of Maxim magazine. Yet she was extremely insecure and felt very unattractive. She was always sabotaging herself and finding excuses to keep her from what she said she wanted to do with her life. She wasn't making the most out of what she had, even though it was a lot more than most have, and people were often envious of her.

My actor friend Harris was commenting on it one day. Out of the blue, he said to me, "She's really had a lot of work done, hasn't she?" I shrugged my shoulders and said, "I guess." This was the first time he'd seen her in a while, and he said, "It looks like she's had even more done since I saw her a couple of years ago." I wasn't sure and just answered, "Maybe?" I thought she looked great. I asked him, "Don't you think it looks good?" I was thinking of her perfect Barbie doll shape with extra full lips and wondering if I'd look better that way. My friend said, "No, it doesn't look good. Insecurity doesn't look good on anyone." I found it fascinating that he would say that, because many guys I know would only see her sexy shape and not care about her inner turmoil. He told me he could tell she didn't like herself, and that was a bigger turn-off than anything she could have looked like before she was filled, lifted, carved, and plumped.

He went on to tell me about this beautiful woman he knew. He described her as strong, confident, and sure of herself. She was a joy to be around, and her smile lit up a room. He said she always made you feel wanted, and she was at peace with how she looked. He told me how attractive he thought it was. I listened, thinking she must have been blessed to already be born with a good earth suit that others would pay for, and that's why she's confident. I asked my friend, "Does she look perfect too?" He said, "No, as a matter of fact, she kind of looks like a wolf and has a large birthmark across more than half of her face, and she doesn't even try to cover it up." What's attractive about his friend is that she's secure in who she is and even able to find joy, and she lavishly spreads it around by always reaching out to people and making gestures of kindness.

Don't Hide Your Light

That really struck me. It got me thinking not only about our acquaintance, but how I must also have come across to people as someone not very attractive—not because of my outside, but because I was projecting how much I didn't love myself. When I hated myself, I wasn't spreading joy around. Sure, I had moments where I was kind, helpful, or giving to others, but not necessarily because their needs were at the forefront of my mind, but because I thought they had more value than I did. When I was inwardly focused on my flaws, I wasn't a vessel pouring out the love of God on others like I should have, like I aim to do now that my eyes aren't constantly on my failures.

Since I'm not wrapped up in the things I think are wrong with me anymore, I can see more clearly when those around me are hurting, and I'm able to help uplift them. Before getting over myself, my inadequacies, and how I looked, I was depressed. I was too self-absorbed to realize how my not loving myself was affecting those around me. Because of it, I couldn't really shine and spread light around to those who needed to see it. Looking back on those times, I'm sad I allowed my perceived shortcomings to consume me.

Even though I had the light of the world living inside me, all I could project was a dim and dull little night light. God said, "You are the light of the world—like a city on a hilltop that cannot be hidden. No one lights a lamp and then puts it under a basket. Instead, a lamp is placed on a stand, where it gives light to everyone in the house. In the same way, let your good deeds shine out for all to see, so that everyone will praise your heavenly Father" (Matthew 5:14-16 NLT). But that's not what I did.

God expected of me to shine His light everywhere I went. Yet in my earthen vessel, what the Bible calls a temple of the Holy Spirit (1 Corinthians 6:19), I wasn't letting His light shine through me. God, in the form of the Holy Spirit Himself, lived inside my temple (my house). The whole neighborhood should've seen me shine with the brightest light. Do you know how bright God is? Revelation says there's no night in Heaven and no need for light, sun or moon, for God will shine upon us (Revelation 22:5, 21:23).

He wanted to shine through me brighter than the noonday sun (Isaiah 58:10, Psalm 37:6, Job 11:17). Listen to this: I had a light in me that was so bright, there would never be a need for any other light source, and nobody knew it, because I chose to have all my blinds down and shutters closed! I didn't open my windows, let anyone in, or let His light shine through and spread warmth on anyone on cold and cloudy nights. I felt that if my blinds were open and people could see into my house, my soul, they'd see everything I didn't want them to see. Even with all God's brightness living in me, I suspected they'd find spiderwebs in every corner, skeletons in every closet, cracks in the foundation, and chipping paint—basically all my flaws.

It hadn't crossed my mind that God's light could cover all my surface dings and inner imperfections better than the brightest lights they blast on stars on the red carpet, which buff out any spot or wrinkle. I thought if people really got to know me, defects and all, they'd flee. I didn't let people in. I wouldn't even let them get close enough to put their face up to the window and try to get a glimpse of what was inside. I pushed people away, wrapping myself in caution tape that said "Do not cross" by my attitude and my behaviors.

When I finally detached who I really was—my spirit—from this vessel I dwell in and all of the maintenance I thought it needed, I was able to reach out and make a difference in many more people's lives. And you too can get to the same place. No matter what you look like, how your body's functioning, or what others think of you, you can be happy, fulfilled, at peace, and moving forward in the unique calling God created you for, and you can make a difference in others for eternity. This separation is important for us in order to live our best life. Scripture urges us, "...Whatever you do, do it for the glory of God" (1 Corinthians 10:31 NLT). Being upset or unhappy about the body God gave you, hiding away, staying shy, not speaking up, and not shining the way your Maker would like you to isn't honoring Him.

When you stand before Him one day and give an account for what you did with your life, you don't want regrets over trivial things. Please honor God, using what He gave you to the best of your abilities, no matter how inadequate you may feel it is. Please don't waste your precious time and resources trying to reclaim what once was, trying to restore these physical things back to what they used to be. Rather, take what God gave you and make the best out of what you've got. When you do, you'll have freedom to enjoy life again. The doors of your soul will swing wide open, and His light will pour out of you. Others will see your beauty from the treasure inside you, and you'll lead them out of their darkness and into God's glorious light.

Chapter Twelve

Are You Really Worthy of God's Love?

Throughout this book, I've been telling you that you are worthy, and teaching you the many reasons why that's true. Everything you've learned from the beginning until now has been building you up and building your belief in who God created you to be and why you have worth. I don't know the specific reason you felt led to pick up this book, but if I were to guess, I'd say it has to do with the question you've been asking yourself for years: *Am I really worthy? How could I be? I know I don't deserve it. I've made far too many mistakes in my life. How could I be worthy if I don't deserve it?*

No matter how many times I've told you who you are and how God feels about you, there's a part of you that still doesn't believe it, or is afraid to believe it. Now is the time to change your thinking. Listen, if you were as bad a person as you think you are, and God thought you shouldn't be here, He'd have already struck you with lightning. I'm kidding, of course, but my point is that you're still here, which means you're redeemable, no matter your faults, failures, or imperfections.

Maybe for years, you've prayed to God for help, and He never seemed to answer (at least not in the way you wanted). You felt unworthy of getting your prayers answered, and that caused you to doubt, and you don't know your doubt is the very thing stopping you. Nothing good can happen when you doubt. Having faith is what pleases God. "But without faith it is impossible to please him" (Hebrews 11:6 KJV). Jesus, even though He was and is God, required people to have faith in order to do the miracles He did. Speaking of His own hometown, where they didn't believe He was the Son of God, Matthew says: "And he did not many mighty works there because of their unbelief" (v. 13:58 KJV). If God tells you something, even if it looks impossible, you must believe it. His scriptures are full of promises He's more than willing to perform for you. Don't slip into doubt just because it's not happening as fast as you'd like it to.

God told Abram to change his name to Abraham, which meant "father of many nations." This was at a time when Abram didn't have any children. He was 99 years old, and his wife was 90, and they couldn't have kids their whole married life. Genesis 18:11 (NKJV) says, "...Sarah had passed the age of childbearing." When Sarah heard these messengers from God tell her husband she'd have a child, she couldn't believe it. So, she laughed. Maybe what I've told you about your worthiness at some point in this book has made you laugh as well.

You might come from a place where you don't feel worthy of His love, His grace, or having your prayers answered because of something you've done or haven't done. Or maybe you've felt like it was impossible, like Sarah, because of your age or some other factor. Maybe you feel like I felt for many years, that there are too many things working against you, and you're not worth much or anything at all, so why would God answer your prayers? And you're right—*if* you're trying to be worthy on your own, through your own ability, or by judging your accomplishments. Are you ready to know for sure, once and for all, that You Are Worthy?

From rash and rich to realization and regret

Let me start by telling you a story about someone who totally screwed up his life and blew everything, to the point he felt there was no coming back.

There was a son who was impatient; he wanted to get out of his dad's house and be his own man. He didn't want to have to wait several more decades for his dad to croak. He wanted his old man's money, his inheritance, and didn't want to wait for pops to be six feet under to get it.

He gets his father to give him his portion of the estate right then. And what does he do with the money? Nothing noble, that's for sure. He doesn't start an orphanage, donate a hospital wing, give to charity, or even buy a house and start a family. No, he goes to some far-off place, like the Las Vegas strip. He blows all his cash on loose living, or prodigal living, which means wasteful, reckless, extravagant spending on things that didn't matter, like having the best food, prime rib and lobster every night. He's popping corks of the most expensive, aged booze, and rolling around on silk sheets and bear-skin rugs with the highest-class hookers his gold coins could buy. And lickety-split, he had nothing left. He blew what his father had worked a lifetime for. He was starving, and there was a famine in the land.

Well, he didn't dare go back to his father like a penitent dog with his tail between his legs and beg. He wasn't going to admit he blew it. He gets a job as the guy who feeds the pigs on somebody's farm. Now this prodigal is starving, so the scraps the pigs are eating look tasty to him. As he's salivating over the pig slop, it finally occurs to him that at his father's house, even the servants have plenty of food left over. He questions himself: "What am I doing hanging out with these pigs eating their orts? Am I nuts? How did I go from the lifestyle of the rich and infamous to pig yards of the poor and forgotten?"

He thinks, "I'll just tell my dad I'm an idiot, I royally screwed up, and I don't deserve to be his kid anymore." (Have you ever felt like that? I know I have. I've said, "God, I really messed up, I don't deserve to be your child anymore.") The prodigal thinks, *I'll ask him if I can just be his servant because even that would be better than living like this.* He realized, like many of us do, what Psalm 84:10 (MSG) says, "I'd rather scrub floors in the house of my God than be honored as a guest in the palace of sin." It's better to be a servant for his dad than even to lead the lavish lifestyle he was living. He thought there was no way he'd be accepted back into his father's house as a son.

Sometimes we feel the same, thinking God wouldn't want us because of the shameful thing we've done. He certainly wouldn't consider us his child anymore. We should just be His servant because we don't deserve anything more. We aren't worthy after what we've done.

But let's see what Jesus has to say in this story, and pick up where the prodigal son has come to his senses in verses 18 through 24 of Luke 15 (Passion Translation): "I want to go back home to my father's house, and I'll say to him, 'Father, I was wrong. I have sinned against you. I'll never be worthy to be called your son. Please, Father, just treat me like one of your employees.'"

"So the young son set off for home. From a long distance away, his father saw him coming, dressed as a beggar, and great compassion swelled up in his heart for his son who was returning home." (It says his father saw him a long distance away, which makes me think his father was out there looking for him, waiting for him, wanting to find him, like your heavenly Father is waiting for you to come, looking for you at a distance to come back to Him, not with anger over what you've done but with a heart swelling with compassion.) "So the father raced out to meet him. He swept him up in his arms, hugged him dearly, and kissed him over and over with tender love. Then the son said, 'Father, I was wrong. I have sinned against you. I could never deserve to be called your son. Just let me be—' The father interrupted and said, 'Son, you're home now!'"

God Wants to Do the Same for You

God wants to interrupt you out of your thoughts that are contrary to how He feels about you; to stop you from even completing the sentence. He doesn't want to hear it when you try to tell Him you aren't worthy. He cuts you off, and what does He do? Does He say, "You can't get your old room back, you're going to have to go live with your aunt or in the servant's quarters for what you did. You're going to get a time out and be grounded, so you can sit and think about what you've done, and come groveling back to me after you've learned your lesson"? No! Here's what his father did and what your heavenly Father wants to do for you: "Turning to his servants, the father said, 'Quick, bring me the best robe, my very own robe, and I will place it on his shoulders. Bring the ring, the seal of sonship, and I will put it on his finger. And bring out the best shoes you can find for my son. Let's prepare a great feast and celebrate. For this beloved son of mine was once dead, but now he's alive again. Once he was lost, but now he is found!'" And everyone celebrated with overflowing joy.

That's exactly how God feels about you. He wants you to come to Him right away, no matter what you've done or how much you've blown it. He's waiting, looking for you with open arms and compassion to embrace you, to lavish you with great love, to treat you like His very own, to put the royal robe on you—His own robe—and the ring which shows everyone you're His child. And He wants to throw a celebration feast for you, in the presence of everyone. He doesn't want to hide you away in case people would judge you, or worry that you've brought shame to the family. Rather, He wants to parade you in front of all to see.

This is very important: You must know He's not ashamed of you. When you come back to Him, He and all the angels are filled with great joy: "...every time one lost sinner repents and turns to him, He says to all his angels, 'Let's have a joyous celebration, for that one who was lost I have found!'" (Luke 15:10 TPT).

That parable really hit home for me, because I once was that prodigal. I strayed from the faith and from the way my parents raised me. I got mixed up with a crowd of people in high school that some would call bad. In hindsight, I believe they were just lost like I was, trying to find meaning and fill their emptiness with whatever seemed cool and rebellious at the time. We broke the law in more ways than one, skipping school, underage drinking, and shoplifting. I didn't think God would want to have anything to do with me—and then I realized, like the prodigal and his father, God still wanted me to come to Him no matter what I'd done, who I was, and what

I'd been through. I didn't need to continue to drown my pain at the bottom of every bottle of alcohol. He was waiting to take away my pain.

I didn't need to feel low and worthless and eat pig scraps. God was there for me, waiting for me, like the father in the story. He was ready to show me my worth and how valuable I was to Him. He saw me slowly starting to come back in my beggar's clothes, ready to grovel, to beg to be a servant. But He ran to greet me and showered me with love and affection. When I repented and accepted His sinless sacrifice in my place, He gave me His robe of righteousness. And when I finally came back to God to confess to Him all the ways I messed up and wasn't worthy, He didn't let me finish the sentence, but told me I was His child. He never once mentioned the lifestyle I was living, never shamed me for wasting my time, money, or life, or brought up any of the bad decisions I made. Instead, He wanted to throw me a celebration; and He wants to do the same for you.

Chapter Thirteen

You May Not Deserve It—But You're Still Worthy

Why have you been confused all these years about your worthiness? Why have you doubted it? Why have you believed the lies from society, the devil, and even yourself, saying you're not worthy or deserving of His love? Perhaps one of the reasons there's confusion is that you've mistaken your worth in God's eyes with whether you DESERVE the title of "worthy."

This was a conversation I had with one of my coaching clients. When I told him he deserved to be happy and have his prayers answered, he went on to correct me and let me know why he didn't actually deserve it. And yes, if you're seeing your worth as something you must earn, then of course, you're not worthy; not a single one of us is.

Part of our confusion is that people often use the word *worthy* and the word *deserving* interchangeably. The dictionary doesn't help bring much clarity, because it gives both words similar meanings. Both definitions mention a person having great merit or being qualified, which might lead us to believe they are something we earn or something we have control over. In the natural, in our human experience, that's what we are used to. Right?

When someone is up for a job promotion, and several people are vying for the same position, the management team will often ask who really deserves this promotion. It'll be based on the person's prior work performance. Did they do the job right, in an efficient manner? Did they perform their tasks with excellence, and bring in the product on time and under cost?

A boss can look at someone and determine whether this person deserves a raise or a promotion or if they don't. However, *a human cannot determine another human's worthiness.*

Even if you're passed up for the job promotion, you're still worthy. Your worth is determined by God alone. It's not based on what you've done but based on what He's done and determined. In God's eyes, you are worthy regardless of whether you've earned it or not.

When it comes to your worthiness, here are a few things you need to know:

You can't earn it.
You don't deserve it.
It's not based on how you feel.
Only God can determine your worth.

You can't earn it

Just like salvation, God's grace, and love, there's nothing you can do to earn your worthiness. God determined you were worthy enough to die for and to redeem while you were at your worst. God did it for you long before you were healed, living clean, problem-free, or tithing. He did it though He knew you would be in despair and depravity during a time when you had no redeemable qualities.

As a matter of fact, He loved you enough to plan this even before the earth was made. Revelation 13:8 calls Jesus the Lamb who was slain *before* the foundation of the world. Before your parents even knew about you, before there was a Red Sea parting, Moses, the Garden of Eden or a living Adam, God knew you would mess up and determined you were worth sacrificing all for.

Your worthiness, besides not being able to be earned, can't be taken away or lessened by what other people do. For instance, have you ever seen some people get really riled up and excited when their favorite sports team is doing well, and they get down in the dumps and depressed when their team is on a losing streak? They are tying how they feel about themselves to what someone else is doing or not doing. Your worthiness is *your* worthiness; it's not linked to any other person or thing, or even linked to any success or failure.

A human cannot determine another human's worthiness.

Here's another example: As parents, we can feel like a lousy parent if our kids behave terribly. We may do everything we know how to do to raise our kids in a godly fashion, and our kids can still make a choice to go out and do silly or dangerous things that have nothing to do with how they were raised.

I saw this firsthand with my own brother, when the school principal was calling my mom almost every day, saying, "I have your son in my office. Do you know what your son did today?" My mom would take a deep breath and say, "I have no idea, but I suppose you're going to tell me." Luckily, my mom was secure enough in who she was not to have her worth as a person or a parent devalued by her son making bad choices. But a lot of people do. I know I've had many moments when my older son Timothy, who is special needs, would act out and behave badly, and I'd feel like somehow it was my fault. People would tell me I'm not disciplining him enough, and I'd feel unworthy or incapable as a parent. But we need to know that what other people choose to do often has nothing to do with us. Nor is it necessarily because of something we've done wrong.

You can't earn your worthiness, because it's not based on your deeds. It's based on whose you are. I know some of you may be thinking, *but what about the verse in James, "...faith without works is dead"?*

Yes, it's true you demonstrate how much you love God by how you act and live, and you are rewarded accordingly for it. But even if you never did a good deed, He counted you worthy. God showed us we have worth we didn't earn by dying for people who didn't even want Him, and who still want nothing to do with Him. In the same way, He sacrificed for you before you knew Him or even cared to seek Him.

The reason we live like we're defeated is because we don't know whose we are. If you don't know who you are, it's easy to get pushed around. But if you are in Christ, the Father is your God, and the Holy Spirit lives inside you; you are worthy. He counts you worthy. Worthy enough for Him to give His life for you, even before you came to faith in Him.

If you serve God, it shouldn't be because you think you have anything to prove, or because you must in order to get into Heaven. There are not enough good deeds you could do to earn Heaven. And no matter how good you think you are, you'll never be good enough (on your own). Romans tells us: "There is none who does good, no, not one" (v. 3:12 NKJV). This isn't just about you not being good enough; outside of Christ alone, there has never lived a person who was good enough on their own, not even Noah and his family, whom God spared when He wiped out everyone else on the earth; Enoch, who walked with God and never had to experience death; or even virgin Mary, who was chosen to be the mother of Jesus.

They all needed God. Not even the forefathers of our faith, Abraham, Isaac and Jacob, were good enough, nor David, who God said was a man after His own heart (1 Sam 13:14). As James tells us: "For the person who keeps all of the laws except one is as guilty as a person who has broken all of God's laws" (James 2:10 NLT). You should serve God because you love Him and you feel compelled to, not because you think it's earning you anything.

For example: Have you ever gotten a gift of money from a relative or a friend? A gift you did nothing to earn; they just wanted to bless you because they love you? I would guess that 99% of the times that someone writes you a check and gives you a monetary gift, you're not going to refuse it or send it back because you don't think you're worthy. You're going to cash the check and use it to better your life and meet your needs.

Your worthiness is like a check God wrote you for a million dollars. It could help you a lot in life—but only if you cash it. If you don't cash it, you'll never get the benefit. It's just like each spiritual gift from God: They're all available to you (without "earning" them); all you have to do is accept them and use them in order to gain the benefits, like cashing the check. But it starts with you believing you are worthy. When you believe it, you'll act like it, and you'll become it.

You don't deserve it

Nope. Me neither. None of us do. Of course you don't deserve it. Only God does. "He alone is your God, the only one who is worthy of your praise…" (Deuteronomy 10:21 NLT). Apart from Him we are nothing, but with Him, we have our worth.

The trouble is, if you don't know you are worthy and think you must be deserving it, you'll never live the life God intended for you, or reap all the benefits there are to reap. Unless you accept that you are worthy, you'll live like someone who doesn't know who they are, who doesn't know their royal heritage. He calls you His child. You ought to live like you are. In 2 Corinthians, He says, "I will be a Father to you, and you shall be My sons and daughters, says the LORD Almighty" (v. 6:18 NKJV).

God wants you to be His child and have childlike faith. "…Unless you are converted and become as little children, you will by no means enter the kingdom of heaven. Therefore whoever humbles himself as this little child is the greatest in the kingdom of heaven" (Matthew 18:3-4 NKJV). It has nothing to do with you "deserving" it; as a matter of fact, it has nothing to do with you at all.

Does a new baby deserve to be fed, clothed, or given shelter? They did nothing to earn it; you could say they don't deserve it; but you do it for them because you love them. You're happy to provide a baby with whatever they need. God is the same way, only much more loving, kind, and generous than we could ever be as a parent.

Have you ever noticed how much confidence and worth a child has? A toddler loves to look in the mirror, to lift up their shirt, pat their round belly and laugh. Young children smile when they see themselves. They don't question their worthiness or their value. They never question our love for them. They don't pinch and disdain their chubby parts or get angry about the shape of their eyes. They're not concerned about having a thigh gap. They don't care if they can't spell *hippopotamus*.

If you tell a little girl she's beautiful, no matter what she looks like, she'll beam and dance around like a princess. You tell a little boy he's strong and brave, even if his arms are skinny noodles, he'll stand like a superhero and flex his muscles and smile like it's true. When I tell my older son Timothy that he's smart or handsome, he doesn't ask if I really mean it; he doesn't argue, telling me all the reasons he isn't. He says, "I know" or "Thank you."

Children don't doubt what you're saying is true. But somehow, you've developed doubt. Doubting yourself isn't something you're born with; you develop it from listening to the wrong voices and comparing yourself to others. It doesn't even cross a kid's mind that you won't make them something to eat when they're hungry. A child doesn't feel like they have to do something to be deserving to get their needs met. They believe they deserve it without doing a single thing to earn it.

My sons Timothy and Elijah know I'm going to feed them as many times a day as they need, pay for their doctor's bills, buy them clothes, and provide for them in every way possible, even if they don't do their chores. As parents, we may feel our children are selfish and think they're entitled. But perhaps we could all learn from their example and believe God when He tells us we're worthy without doing a thing to earn it or deserve it.

You may not always understand how God could love you unconditionally, especially when it's impossible for you to have the depth of love for people, even your family, that God has for you. But if your five-year-old breaks your grandmother's heirloom dish, you may be upset for a while, but you don't cast your child away forever because of it.

Yet sometimes, you think God will do that to you when you make a mistake. Here's what God says to you through the prophet Jeremiah: "Yes, I have loved you with an everlasting love; Therefore with lovingkindness I have drawn you" (v. 31:3 NKJV). Everlasting is never-ending; it's forever, nonstop love. And it has no contingencies, meaning it's not dependent upon you fulfilling a bunch of conditions or meeting any requirements. If you break one of his heirloom dishes, even if you break one of his children, and commit whatever you think is the worst crime possible, God still has it within Him to forgive you. I talk more extensively about that in my upcoming book and online course, *You Are Loved.*

Here's the point: You don't deem your child worthy based on whether or not they do their chores. You may bless them with more rewards if they do, but you don't withhold love from your child if they don't. If your child does whatever you think is the worst thing they could do—get hooked on drugs, have a teen pregnancy, drink and drive and kill someone—you are grieved over their decision, yes. But you don't stop loving them. Your human love is fallible, temperamental, and impatient. God's love is not. Isaiah says: "Can a woman forget her nursing child, and not have compassion on the son of her womb? Surely they may forget, Yet I will not forget you" (v. 49:15 NKJV).

It's not based on how you feel

Your worth isn't based on how you feel about yourself. *You Are Worthy* whether you feel like you are or not. Very often, feelings aren't based on anything that's real. For instance, let's say you're feeling fear. True fear is usually based on impending danger or pain. But if you feel afraid to walk onto a stage and give a speech, your life's not in danger; there's no lion coming to eat you; you won't be impaled and die (though someone might throw some rotten tomatoes at you). The only thing that could actually be hurt is your feelings.

Fear, in that case, is only a feeling. And often, we give more credence to feelings than we should. Feelings are fleeting if we let them go quickly past us, or they stick longer if we dwell on them. No matter how long we dwell on a certain feeling, though, it doesn't make it the truth (although you certainly can convince yourself about things that aren't true). I did that for many years regarding my worth and abilities.

There was an Oscar-winning film called *A Man for All Seasons* based on the real life of Sir Thomas More. Sir Thomas was a judge in the courts of England at the time of Henry VIII. He was known as one of the most honest men in the country and wouldn't hesitate to tell people the truth whether they wanted to hear it or not. Henry VIII was power-hungry. He was the King of England, but he also wanted to be head of the Catholic Church. Being King wasn't enough. What stood in the way of that goal was that he wanted to divorce his wife of 20 years and marry a young hottie.

At the time, the Catholic church didn't allow divorce; it was considered a sin. But the King thought, if I get an annulment, it won't count as a divorce. The Church wouldn't grant his annulment because to get a marriage annulled, you had to have had no sexual relations with your spouse. Well, King Henry was married to his wife for 20 years and had kids by her. But he FELT he was above the law and tried to pressure Sir Thomas More (who was later made a saint) to go along with it. Thomas wouldn't be pressured to go against the rules of the Church and comply with the elite by giving his OK to the King, just because the King felt the rules should change for him.

Sir Thomas used this allegory to make his point: "Some say the earth is round; others say the world is flat. If the world is flat, will the King's command make it round? And if it is round, will the King's command flatten it?" In other words, is how the King feels about his rights and his own importance going to change what is so? No. Your feelings don't determine if you're worthy, because what's so is what's so. Just because you feel unworthy doesn't change the truth that you are worthy. God already said you are, so it comes down to this: are you going to believe God, or call Him a liar?

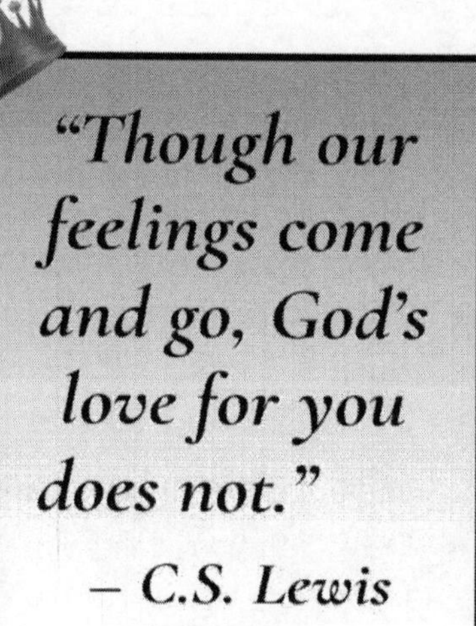

One of the reasons we don't feel worthy is that we often compare ourselves to others. We see others behaving better, doing more for God, being more productive for the kingdom, or being more charitable, and we assume they have more value to God than we do. Yet your worth can't be compared to others'. It's not a game or a contest of who's worthy and who's not.

You may be surprised to learn that the saint who feeds the hungry on skid row every Saturday out of his or her own paycheck has the same worth and intrinsic value in God's eyes as the serial killer in prison whom God has forgiven. You are worthy because He chose you before the foundation of the world. He wanted to redeem mankind, and He knew you and I would need it. He determined that you were worthy before you were even born and set a plan in place to offer His Son on your behalf before He formed the earth.

No matter what anyone thinks about you,

> ***"Your value doesn't decrease based on someone's inability to see your worth."*** —Unknown

Your worth can't be lessened based on people's thoughts about you, including your own.

Our society, sometimes even you yourself, may not deem people as valuable if they, for instance, are old, can't work anymore, are special needs, or aren't "a productive member of society." But that doesn't make them any less valuable in God's eyes.

If we treat someone as if they're more worthy than another based on their looks, abilities, or output, we are not acting in accordance with how God would act. We're creating an atmosphere of divisiveness when we lightly esteem one person and greatly esteem another solely based on their accomplishments, when both have been redeemed by Christ equally. "So why do you condemn another believer? Why do you look down on another believer? Remember, we will all stand before the judgment seat of God" (Romans 14:10 NLT).

Also, when people speak of worth, a lot of times, it has to do with what material value you perceive the person or object to have. You think about what something's worth and how much value something has each time you go to the store and make your purchasing decisions. You wouldn't pay $200 for a can of soup and think it's a good value, but you might think a dress or a suit is worth that much.

If a can of soup drops on the ground and gets a dent, it goes to the clearance rack. If the dress or suit gets a snag or tear in the store, it gets a significant markdown. The price for a $3 can of soup or a $200 dress may be cut in half. According to the salespeople, it doesn't deserve to be sold at full price once it's no longer pristine. It loses some of its value. But God doesn't treat us like a product and demoralize us that way.

He doesn't use a legalistic system when He determines worth. It's not based on what you've accomplished or been through. "God bought you with a high price" (1 Corinthians 6:20 NLT). As a matter of fact, He didn't care that you were torn up, stained, dented, rotting, and shoved onto a clearance rack by someone who had no business judging you. Some may say you didn't even deserve the clearance rack and may have put you in the trash bin. Yet wherever you were when God found you, He didn't pay clearance price for you; He paid full price. He didn't send a holy angel to take your place (of which He had thousands). Rather, He paid with His one and only Son.

"For while we were still weak, at the right time Christ died for the ungodly. For one will scarcely die for a righteous person—though perhaps for a good person one would dare even to die—but God shows his love for us in that while we were still sinners, Christ died for us" (Romans 5:6-8 ESV).

Only God can determine your worth

You could try to tell God you're a terrible, unworthy person all day long, but if you've repented and received His Son, He's going to look at you like He has no idea what you're talking about. Kind of like the look I give to my friends who are size 2 when they complain, "Oh, I'm fat, I need to tone up." You just want to knock some sense into them. (Well, at least I do anyway.)

When we go around complaining that we're not good enough or we don't have what it takes, God shakes His head, probably wanting to knock some sense into us and ask us,

"Don't you know who you are?" Colossians tells us, "...For in Christ lives all the fullness of God in a human body. So you also are complete through your union with Christ..." (v. 2:9-10 NLT). If you have God, you're complete. You don't need anything else—to have a certain degree, come from the perfect family, have a huge number in your bank account, belong to a special society or club, or have the right BMI and muscle-to-fat ratio. You don't need anything other than what you have found in your partnership with God's Son.

Whether you think or feel you're worthy is irrelevant

"Remember therefore how you have received and heard; hold fast and repent. ... and they shall walk with Me in white, for they are worthy." "He who overcomes shall be clothed in white garments, and I will not blot out his name from the Book of Life; but I will confess his name before My Father and before His angels" (Revelation 3:3-5 NKJV). If you're worthy enough to live in Heaven for eternity, and have Jesus confess your name before the angels, you are worthy to live that way on Earth before mankind, because it's God who has determined you are worthy, not man. If you're not living like you're worthy, and constantly putting yourself down and pointing out your faults, you're going against God's wishes. You can't keep tearing down what He's trying to build up, and that's you!

Isn't it time you believed God when He tells you who you are—that you are worthy, chosen, and loved? I know some people will give compliments and say things they don't mean, but God doesn't. You can tell He means it by His actions.

Matthew talks about the pearl of great price. "…The kingdom of heaven is like a merchant seeking beautiful pearls, who, when he had found one pearl of great price, went and sold all that he had and bought it" (v. 13:45-46 NKJV). You are a pearl of great price. God gave up everything for you, yet the enemy tried to devalue you. He tried all these years to tell you that you weren't worth anything. Yet what makes you valuable, worthy, and priceless is how much God thought you were worth—to leave His deity, come to Earth to give you an example of how to live, and ultimately to pay the cost for everything you've ever done wrong and will do wrong. That's the kind of love He has for you; that's why you must know you are worthy.

You can't keep tearing down what God is trying to build up, and that's you!

If you want to discover why you have not been able to see yourself the way God sees you … read on.

Chapter Fourteen

God-Colored Glasses

Throughout this book, I've told you how amazing you are, but still you may not believe it. You're stuck believing you're no good, and you don't have what it takes. You're still looking for your miracle cologne that will make you attractive to people, or the magic elixir that'll make them like you. You might be a little bit stubborn like I was, needing a bit more insight to help you rip those muddy lenses off your face and really start seeing yourself the way God does. Here's where you need to take the action steps to make that happen.

I shared with you the way God sees you so you could begin to see yourself that way too. In this chapter, I'll bring the idea of how to see yourself the way God does full circle.

The reason you still can't see yourself the way He does is that you don't yet know that you can't see. You may think the way you're viewing yourself and what you see in front of you is the truth. But you can't see your true self yet if you're looking through a pair of dirty, tainted lenses. Your vision is blurred, nothing makes sense, and it's hard to see how it will all work out. Discouragement sets in.

If you walk outside and your glasses are gunked up, you can't properly perceive the shining sun; everything may look grey and gloomy. You know if we're speaking about a physical pair of glasses, you need to wash them to see properly. But what you don't know is that you have inner lenses that are tainted, and they affect your thought life. You may have a negative thought life based on what you see, not knowing your vision is skewed. You may say, "I know I'm not good enough. Why can't you see it?" But what if what you see isn't reality? In all likelihood, you've had these negative thoughts about yourself for so many years, you don't even remember putting those inner lenses on. You think how you see yourself is correct. You argue, "I see perfectly fine," but you don't know you're wearing lenses, let alone that they're dirty.

To make it clearer, for example, if the lenses you put on are green and I tell you I'm wearing a white shirt, you will argue with me all day long, telling me my shirt is green. Heck, I may have red lenses on, and I think I'm wearing a red shirt because when I look in the mirror, that's what I see. Then in a real-life scenario, you and I get into an argument over our different points of view. We fight over our perspective about ourselves, other people, politics and different situations, and how we see the world. You're arguing that I'm wearing a green shirt, I'm arguing that it's red, and we don't know we're both wrong. Neither of us is seeing accurately. Only God and those seeing through God-colored glasses can tell us the shirt is white. Until we remove the dirty, wrong-colored lenses, we won't see properly.

There are a couple of reasons why you may not believe someone when they tell you you're not seeing yourself in the proper perspective. First, the feedback can't just come from anyone. It's got to be someone you trust—a mentor, a true friend, someone you look up to, someone who has never steered you wrong. Second, it must come at the right time, when you're ready to make a change—when you're tired of living the way you've been living, tired of hating the person staring back at you from the mirror, tired of underestimating yourself, and you're ready to move beyond what you think you can do and who you think you are.

When you take off your worldly lenses—the ones that see and measure the way the world does and that judge by outward appearance and a skewed perspective—and put on God-colored glasses, only then are you able to regain your sight. When you see clearly (according to what God's word says about *you*), it's much easier to walk by faith and take a leap into your desired future.

If you could look at a situation the way God would look at a situation and have that kind of discernment, it would save you a lot of heartache. You wouldn't have as many problems in life if you were seeing through the right lenses.

I used to be made fun of for my eyes and my voice. Now I'm recognized in a positive way for both. Why shouldn't that happen for you? You may discover that some traits you don't like about yourself—things you think are "flaws" or "weaknesses"—are just the things that could bring you the greatest success and skyrocket you to levels higher than you ever thought you could go.

You used to love yourself

If you can, I want you to remember back to a time in your life when appearances didn't matter to you. There was that window of time (often shorter than it should have been), where you did what you wanted, regardless of others' opinions. You would run around the house in your underwear, belting out your favorite song with a hairbrush or a spoon microphone. You'd sing, dance, smile, and bang out songs on your mom's pots and pans. You never cared about the number on the scale, the label on your clothes, the zeros in your bank account, your IQ, or "fitting in."

Back then, you were carefree. Anything you wanted to do was possible for you. You were happy, able to love yourself and express yourself without fear … until, one day, somebody or several people with a false sense of identity, who didn't know they were made in God's image and who were not seeing through God-colored glasses—or maybe were just hurting so much themselves that their vision of everything (including you) was skewed—said or did things to you that made you question who you were, what you were capable of, and what your place was in the world. They slowly started to break your little spirit down. They left you in a state of being unsure of who you were supposed to be but totally convinced that who you were was not good enough.

If you take two children and you tell one every day, "You're a loser, you shouldn't have been born, you never do anything right," and you take another and tell them, "You're a winner, you were born to fulfill your destiny, you can accomplish anything you set out to do"—which child do you think is going to be more successful and able to handle whatever challenges come their way? Which one do you think will see themselves in a way that honors who God created them to be? Dumb question, right? But not to the one crippled by the bad input. Most of the time, it's going to be the one programmed with the correct messaging who will be able to move forward. The reason is, the programming they received is the lens through which they see themselves and everyone and everything around them. Unfortunately, bad and false "input" can be just as effective in programming us as good and true input.

Often, unless you make a very concentrated effort to change, whatever programming you had as a child continues into adulthood as you solidify it and program yourself the way you were taught. What you speak about yourself long enough, you eventually believe. Telling myself thousands of times through my teens and 20s that I was ugly and fat resulted in my vision being skewed. Honestly, I'd lost sight altogether about what was true, which made me only see fat and ugly when I looked in the mirror, regardless of what was actually there. Very early in life, I'd picked up the world's warped and smudged lenses and put them on, and I didn't even realize it. You did too, which is why you've lost sight of your worth and aren't seeing correctly.

Blind no more

You may have heard the Indian parable about the blind men and the elephant. It's about a group of men with visual impairment who've never come across an elephant before. They try to figure out what the elephant is by touching it, each in a different place. Then they do their best to describe what they think it is. The one touching its legs feels as if it's a sturdy tree; the one leaning against its side feels as if it's a wall; the one touching its ear thinks it's a fan; the one feeling the trunk thinks it's a massive snake; the one holding its tail thinks it's a whip; and the one holding its tusk thinks it's a spear. In some versions, each man begins to believe the others are lying, and they all end up in a big fistfight!

The point is, we humans tend to claim absolute truth based on our limited, subjective experiences. Each opinion or thought might seem true for that person, but often it's not the whole picture. We don't really know what is going on based on our limited experience, just like someone who's blind and has never heard of an elephant can't understand what an elephant is by only the one area they're touching. The kind of life you live and how you see yourself when you're seeing through the world's dirty lenses isn't the whole picture, especially when you're only focusing on what you feel are your faults.

Like the blind man holding the trunk of the elephant, if this elephant wraps his trunk around the man, this man may be scared to death that his life is in danger, as if he's about to get squeezed to death and then swallowed alive by a massive snake. He doesn't realize he's touching part of an animal that's actually a vegetarian. And when you don't see your life clearly, you too may think you're about to get eaten. You end up living a fearful, broken life; a blurred life, where you're not reaching your full potential, and you're not able to see past the smudges you think you have, to effectively look at your future and see that it's bright.

You can't see the sunshine through the haze, or catch a glimpse of the divine purpose and plan for you, when you've got mucked-up glasses from believing lies you've held on to all your life, whether those thoughts are from the opinions of others slipping in, or the devil planting those thoughts in your mind, or even your own voice because of how defeated you may feel. Perhaps you've been comparing your abilities and looks to someone else's abilities and looks. When you do that, you don't even recognize your good traits, and can't see how far you've come.

You're blinded to what you can accomplish and what you're capable of just the way you are with the resources, brains, and body you have, which are more than enough for you to accomplish any dream you can imagine, with God's help. When you continue to see through the world's lenses, you stifle yourself, and you're not living in your full purpose. You're not happy, and you'll never be satisfied.

You must break those toxic lenses off your spiritual eyes to see clearly. The most effective way to do that is to find out what God says about you. If you're a believer and you believe the word of God, you know God can't lie: "And he who is the Glory of Israel will not lie…" (1 Samuel 15:29 NLT). You know whatever He says is the truth, and that truth doesn't just apply to other people; it applies to you too.

When God tells you that He'll make you the head and not the tail, and you will be above only and not beneath (Deuteronomy 28:13), and He will give you the desires of your heart (Psalm 37:4), you're obliged to believe Him. Even if you don't feel worthy, even if you don't see how it's true, even if you don't think you have what it takes to accomplish the dreams in your heart, you have to take Him at His word. It's not that your life won't be without trials once you discover your worth, but God will help you overcome each one, just as He's overcome the whole world (John 16:33). He's got a big purpose and calling for you.

"No good thing does he withhold from those who walk uprightly" (Psalm 84:11 ESV). It doesn't say "only in Heaven."

Scripture actually tells us, "…your will be done, on earth as it is in heaven" (Matthew 6:10 ESV). There are many scriptures that tell you how blessed you'll be if you obey what the word of God has to say. This is one: "If you are willing and obedient, you will eat the best of the land" (Isaiah 1:19 NASB). God says, "But you are a chosen race, a royal priesthood, a holy nation…" (1 Peter 2:9 ESV). Do you hear that? God said you're *royalty*. Isn't it time you accept that?

If you're still groveling on the ground, please stop. See the impact you could have on your life, your dreams, and this world. Stop seeing through worldly lenses where you compare how you stack up in matters that are inconsequential—the things that will burn up, shrivel away and rust (your looks, your talent, your bank account, your accomplishments, your physical ability, your IQ); all the things that don't matter in the long run. You're robbing yourself of your true identity.

Next, let me show you how to get rid of the worldly view in order to regain your SIGHT.

Chapter Fifteen

How to Regain Your SIGHT

If you want to have more happiness and turn around every area of your life, you'll have to change how you see things. To do that, I've developed a 5-step formula I call "The SIGHT Method" to help you.

Let's start off with S:

"S" is for *See*

You really need to SEE everything you are doing. Notice the things you are saying. You've got to recognize your habits, your dialog with others and with yourself. Observe how you react in every situation. What makes you frustrated? What causes you anxiety? When do you lash out? When do you hide from others and not engage? Take note of these things. When I say take note, I mean for real. Go ahead and write them down. This is a very important first step. Because you can't fix anything if you're unwilling to acknowledge or admit it, you must know what you're saying and doing and how you're reacting. Grab a pen and paper, and let's get started.

If you're not sure where to begin or what it might look like for you as you're making your list, you may write down some things like, "I was impatient with my kids," "I snapped at my spouse when he asked me to help around the house," "I lost my temper at the grocery store when someone cut in front of me," "When I saw someone I didn't want to talk to, I avoided them," "While shopping for clothes, I put myself down and ridiculed myself, saying I was fat and ugly when the clothes didn't fit right, and got discouraged," "I told myself I was going to go on a diet and only have smoothies and salads for breakfast and lunch, but I went through the drive-through again," "My co-worker brought donuts to work, and I gave in. Then I told myself over and over again the rest of the day how I'd never reach my weight goal, and I couldn't do anything right," or "I had the opportunity to ask my boss for a raise, but I clammed up and didn't say anything."

I want you to write down these kinds of behaviors so you can see and acknowledge them, yes, as a start. However, a list with only negatives isn't what you should focus on when you're trying to get over self-worth issues, i.e., only seeing your bad traits. You need to see your positive traits as well. You may have been programmed to be blind to any good things about your own characteristics, actions, or words, but you've got to start to SEE them. Acknowledging the things you may be doing right is not "prideful"; it's just *truthful.* And that truthfulness is the next step in the SIGHT method.

Some of these things you do or say may seem insignificant, and you may be thinking, *Why should I write this down?* But they aren't insignificant. To get to the heart of what is working and what isn't—to see accurately—all those things should be noted. For example, "I gave my daughter the biggest, longest hug today and told her I was proud of her," "I held my spouse's hand when we were out for a walk and told him I was grateful for him," "I let an elderly person take the closer parking spot even though I was there first," "I told the sales clerk she had a beautiful smile," "I helped a co-worker with her report that was due," "When my boss said I did a good job, I said thank you, and didn't try to point out all the ways I thought I should have done it better," "I ordered a side salad to go with my burger instead of fries," and "I planned a date night with my spouse, and we finally got to have a much-needed heart-to-heart talk."

Our days aren't going to look all negative or all positive, but some kind of crazy mix of both. But without this first step of seeing all that you're doing and saying and how you're responding, you can't take the next critical step.

There's a reason why, when you get a trainer or a weight loss coach, they want you to track every bite of food you eat and all your activity—to see what you need to change to reach your goals more quickly. When you identify specific areas like I just did in your ways of being, acting, and speaking, you can see where you struggle and where you do well. Then it becomes easier to pinpoint the behavior that does or doesn't serve your true identity or purpose.

Another note: Be as specific as you can. I find this works better than being general, like saying, "I always put myself down," or, "I help people." That's harder to wrap your head around when you're ready to make some changes. You need to know specifically what you say when you put yourself down, and how you help people, and with what?

Did you make your list? If you want to get some freedom, it's important that you don't just read about this exercise, but that you actually do it. You'll gain far more from doing the exercise than you ever will reading about it. Go ahead and SEE everything you've done over the last few days that you can remember, and write it all down. Don't worry, I'll be waiting right here when you come back.

~ ~ ~ *(Please don't skip this step. Write it all down!)* ~ ~ ~

How did you do? Do you have a long list? I know I did when I did this exercise.

Once you can see all that you're doing—the good, the bad and the ugly—only then can you move on to the next step to regain your sight.

"I" is for *Inspect*

You're going to inspect what in your way of being, acting, or speaking should be kept, and what behaviors, words, thoughts, or beliefs you should reject.

How do you do that?

After you *see* what you've been doing and have your list, let's *inspect* it and ask some questions. With everything on your list, ask yourself, *Is this self-talk serving me? Is this habit helping me? Does my behavior make me feel empowered and confident to live to my fullest potential, or does it just make me feel bad? Does how I'm acting strengthen my relationships or tear them down?* You must constantly assess your thoughts and ask, *When I believe this, or do this, does it make me excited and motivated to go after my dreams? Or does it drag me down and make me not want to get out of bed? Or does it just make me feel like, "Why bother with my goals? I'll just watch TV every night after work"? Am I spending more time building other people's dreams and sabotaging my own?* The Inspect phase is where you'll dissect and start to discern the behaviors and practices which serve, help, and empower you.

If you're not sure if your thoughts, words, or behaviors are a problem, or they just seem neutral and you can't really tell if they're good or bad, or if they are helping you or hurting you, ask yourself this: *What would God say about me? Is this how He'd look at me or this situation? Is this how He would treat me or others? Is this what He'd focus on?* Remember, "As a man thinks in his heart, so is he" (Proverbs 23:7). We must be mindful of the thoughts that run through our heads, because we become what they are.

An old proverb says, "You can't stop a bird from flying over your head, but you can stop it from building a nest in your hair." You may not know this, but not every thought you think is the truth. Some of your thoughts are coming from God or the Holy Spirit speaking to you; some are from you (which, if your programming is bad, or you've not removed your worldly lenses, may hurt you, not help you); but some are planted by the evil one. It's your job to *Inspect* them and decipher which is which. If they're not from God, and they're not giving you courage to live your purpose powerfully, don't let them make a home in your mind.

Even if you think when you put yourself down that you're "just being honest," please remember that some of your thoughts may contain elements that are true or partially true, but if you use those "true" thoughts to belittle or berate yourself, then it's not helpful, it's harmful.

Here's an example: You may constantly call yourself "fat," and it may be a fact that you're carrying some extra, unhealthy weight on your body, but calling yourself "fat" can often be a value judgment. When you say, "I'm fat," it's an identity statement as if that's who you are. But it's not. It's only a condition your body is currently in. It's NOT WHO YOU ARE. It's a whole different thing to say, "The doctor says my body (not me) is clinically obese, so I need to shed some pounds for my health and longevity." Do you see how the first one makes you feel terrible about yourself because you've used an "I AM" (as if it is you and you feel helpless to change it), but the second is about YOUR BODY (not yourself), which might empower you to make some strides to help your health and ultimately even make you feel better about yourself? Your body's not even who you are; it's just an earth suit you're currently residing in. Since you are a speaking spirit living IN a body, it's impossible for YOU to be fat.

You need to know the difference between what God has to say and what the world or society that has indoctrinated you since birth has to say on a topic. You can do this through knowing His word. You may not have read the entire Bible before or know all that God has to say on any specific topic. The beauty of living in this era is you have the Internet search engines at your fingertips. You can type in, "What does scripture say about ____________," then just fill in the blank for any subject you want to know about.

This is very important, because you may think what you've heard or been raised to believe all your life is right. What you've been taught may seem correct, but God doesn't think the way you do, and what you think is right may not be.

Do you ever feel like you don't need God's opinion, like you can figure it out on your own? I have, and I still do sometimes. But when I try to do things my way, sometimes it works, and sometimes it doesn't. Even those times where it works, though, the result is never as good as it would've been had I asked God for guidance, because we don't know everything. If you think something's right for you, you still need to get God's take on the matter to see if your thoughts agree with His. Doing that can save you from a lot of heartache.

Here are some examples of how God's vision is different from how we see things and what we've been taught by the ways of the world:

The world says, "Children should be seen and not heard."

God says, "Let the children come to me, and do not hinder them; for to such belongs the kingdom of heaven" (Matthew 19:14 RSV).

The world says, "Ignorance is bliss."

God says, "My people are destroyed for lack of knowledge" (Hosea 4:6 KJV).

The world says, "If you've got it, flaunt it."

God says, "…dress modestly, with decency and propriety, adorning [your]selves, not with elaborate hairstyles or gold or pearls or expensive clothes, but with good deeds appropriate for women who profess to worship God" (1 Timothy 2:9-10 NIV).

You can see how sometimes what the world has to say may sound logical or right, but when you compare it to God's word, there's a stark contrast.

You know now that you're not the body you live in. But neither are you any of the names or labels people have put on you. You are not their opinions or ideas about you. Those ideas are things that live in your head or other people's heads, but they are not the truth about you. They're merely perceptions. Whenever you're seeking advice or listening to another's opinion, how do you know if the person you're listening to is seeing clearly? Can you trust that they haven't at some point put on a pair of dirty lenses and are giving you advice or a critique based on their skewed vision?

You need insight that's holy and pure, cleansed and filtered by God's word and His thoughts towards you, and not anyone else's opinion. Once you've Inspected all that you're doing, saying and thinking, we move to the letter G.

"G" is for *Garbage*

You're going to get rid of the garbage. This is where you draw a line in the sand and say, "No more!" You stop dwelling on and speaking over your life things that are not beneficial to you. I don't care if you've had 54 different relationships that didn't work out; you're not allowed to call yourself a failure or say you're not good enough to get married and no one will ever want you. If you weigh 400 pounds, you're not allowed to refer to yourself as a fat slob who will never lose weight or be healthy no matter what you try. Even if you think what you're saying is the truth, you must decide from here on out: *I will only speak words that are kind to myself. I won't be at war with myself any longer.* "Let no corrupt communication proceed out of your mouth, but that which is good to the use of edifying, that it may minister grace unto the hearers" (Eph. 4:29 KJV). "The hearers" includes YOU!

Please stop breaking God's heart day after day by calling His favorite creation (you) unworthy in any way. You must get rid of that garbage.

Starting way back in high school, I thought fixing my outside would make me happy. But I didn't realize where I needed the most work was on my inside. I would trash-talk myself, filling myself up with garbage thoughts. I always believed what I was saying, which meant my actions followed suit. However, as an adult, a few years ago, my eyes were opened to how I had been behaving and why I was never able to reach my goals. It all had to do with the mantra running through my head, which was garbage like, "I'm not smart enough, or good enough," etc. Because that's what I thought in my heart, that's who I became.

Rather than reaching my goals as an actor, I was sabotaging myself. I'd run myself ragged trying to do everything else to help on the set because I was convinced that on my own, I couldn't possibly be good enough as an actor for them to hire me. When I booked an acting job, I would tell the producer or director, "I also do makeup, I can do PA work, help produce the film, pick up the food," etc. Many times, they happily accepted my double duty because they were on a budget, and I never asked to be paid to do those extra things. Most of the time, for the first seven or eight years as an actor, I never asked to be paid for my acting work either. Then, of course, wearing all those other hats made my performance as an actor suffer because I couldn't give the role I was playing the full attention it needed. Instead of thinking I needed to do four other people's jobs to be worthy of mine, I simply needed to get rid of the garbage thought that my acting skills alone weren't enough. I should have realized I was good enough when they hired me.

Are you aware of any self-deprecating slogans or self-talk running through your head? What are they? Really search for them. If they don't come to mind right away, ask yourself, *What is it I say to myself or believe that stops me from going for my goals, or even just liking myself? What keeps me from being carefree, letting loose, having fun, or asking that person if they want to be friends? What keeps me from standing up for myself and loving myself the way I am?* Why not grab that pen and paper and make this list right now? What's the garbage you are holding on to? It's important to keep recognizing these patterns. Be honest with yourself about what you say and believe, because it determines what you experience in life. Where you are now is in large part due to the things you've said and believed, whether for good or bad.

Now that you've identified the garbage to get rid of, let's move on to the letter H.

"H" is for *Helpful*

You've got to hold on to what's helpful. What if you only put good stuff in your mind and your heart? What if when you hit a traffic jam or a detour, you didn't automatically say, "Oh great, bad stuff is always happening to me, now I'm going to be late for my meeting," but rather said, "Oh my goodness, I don't know why this is happening, but I know God works all things together for my good, which means this must be some kind of protection for me."

What if, when you ask a girl out and she says no, you stop thinking to yourself, "I'm a loser. No one is ever going to like me. I need to be more handsome or have more money to attract a woman," and say instead, "Lord, I don't know why she said no to me, but I'm going to trust you. You know what you're doing, and if you're keeping her from me, then she wasn't the best you had for me, and you've got someone better for me to date, or marry."

I had to do this myself every time I went to an audition and didn't book the role. Before I got my revelation of self-worth, I would say, "I'm not pretty enough," "They didn't like me," "I'm not a good actor," "Why am I even bothering?" or "I have to lose weight." I had to change my thought life to, "Okay, God, You knew I wanted this acting job, but something about it must not have been right for me. Please help me audition for and book the right jobs. Lead me to the jobs where they'll embrace me for who I am and appreciate the talent I bring to the project. Thank You for the plans You have for me, for good and not for evil, for giving me a future and a hope" (Jeremiah 29:11). "I'm trusting that if I delight myself in You, You will bring me the desires of my heart" (Psalm 37:4).

To hold on to what's helpful, I must challenge you to believe the best. What's the alternative? To be miserable and depressed because you're believing the worst? You don't know what will eventually happen in your life or how everything will turn out. You don't always know what's true. If you have a choice to believe the worst things about yourself or your situation or believe the best, which one is going to make you miserable? Which one is going to give you hope? Go with the hope. There are enough forces of the enemy coming against you to keep you down; why make it worse?

You can't get your heart broken or feel like a loser every time someone says no to you. It isn't helpful. When someone says something negative about you, that doesn't make it the truth; it's just their opinion. That traffic jam you got into may have happened to save you from a car accident. That girl saying "no" may be saving you from a lot of drama and heartache.

When I'm told "no" for an acting job, sometimes it's for the best. I don't know, for instance, what tragedy I may have avoided by not going to set. Conversely, we often don't realize until it happens what beautiful thing we may be able to be there for as a result of what we feel at the time is a disappointment, or a lost opportunity.

Several years ago, I brought my older son, who was two at the time, to his doctor to ask why he wasn't walking yet. That's when I found out he had cerebral palsy. The doctors and therapists heartbreakingly told me he would never walk.

Later, when my son was three and a half, I had auditioned for a film. It was a role I really wanted, but I didn't get it. Then one day, when I knew the film was shooting, I remember being bummed out, thinking, *Man, I could have been on set filming that cool movie, and instead, I'm stuck home on mommy duties.* The day I was "stuck" at home was the day Timothy walked for the first time on his own without the use of a walker. With tears of joy, I was there to witness that miracle! That joyful moment when Timothy defied what the doctors and therapists believed was possible is a memory that can never be replaced or taken from me. What if I had been on that movie set that day? What if I missed that experience because I THOUGHT I knew where I needed to be, doing what I thought I was missing out on? It turned out I was exactly where I was supposed to be.

How many times have you wished to be somewhere else and yet, you are exactly where you are for reasons that are still unfolding, that you don't understand just yet? I tell you that story because you've got to get to the point where you trust God, where you know He's going to work everything out for your good (Romans 8:28), and where you believe He knows better than you do. Even if you're going through a difficult time and you're in pain, and don't understand why something is happening—maybe the devil has attacked you or your family or your finances—you must trust that God can and will turn it around, and know He wishes above all things that you would prosper and be in good health, even as your soul prospers (3 John 2). When you have that level of acceptance around things you may want but can't control … that's when miracles appear.

Until I bathed in the word of God, I couldn't cleanse those lenses properly. Imagine what your life would look like if you only put positive thoughts into your psyche and what the word of God has to say. Decide right now to stop the negative self-talk, the detrimental thoughts, and to speak and dwell only on "…whatever is true, whatever is noble, whatever is right, whatever is pure, whatever is lovely, whatever is admirable—if anything is excellent or praiseworthy—think about such things" (Philippians 4:8 NIV). These are the kinds of things that will help you hold on to what's helpful. When you start to speak and think on these things, you may of course not believe them right away. But commit to saying and thinking about them until you do. If you do this, you'll eventually be totally transformed, just like the scripture says: "…be transformed by the renewing of your mind" (Romans 12:2 NKJV).

Which brings us to the letter T.

"T" is for *Training*

You have to train your brain for gain! Just like a computer, it's all about the programming; what goes in is what is going to come out.

I believed my programming, my "I'm not smart enough" chants. It resulted in my own confusion and the automatic assumption that most things were too complicated for me. That way of thinking became who I was. When an opportunity presented itself and it required me to learn something new, I would sabotage the opportunity because I didn't believe I was able to learn anything new. If I had to change the format on a video I was uploading for an audition or something technical like that, I wouldn't even attempt to figure it out. I would block myself even from reading an instruction booklet or watching a tutorial because I was convinced that I wouldn't understand it. So I was annoying my husband and everyone around me, always asking them to help me with every little technical thing, since I had (mis)trained my brain to reject the possibility that I could figure it out.

Have you ever done anything like that? Have you robbed yourself of opportunities because of how you programmed your brain to think? What garbage have you been training your brain to dwell on? What kinds of thoughts do you repeat until it causes anxiety that takes your brain and body hostage? Have you missed out on joy because you didn't know the right way to think? What kinds of things were you upset about or not happy with God about because you couldn't understand the bigger plan? Are you willing to keep living in a way that's unfulfilling, painful, and depressing? If not, let's talk about how to train your brain.

The reason you made the lists of the good you're doing and the not-so-good you're doing isn't to feel pain and be reminded of how terrible you are, but to see what you're saying and doing that needs to be reset.

When I looked at my list, I saw that one of the things I did was say "no" to my little Elijah, who wanted to play outside, because I had computer work to get done. When I started to examine how he could be happy, and I could be happy too, I realized I could've taken my laptop computer outside and gotten work done while I watched him play, and not have him stuck in the house watching cartoons while I worked. Part of training our brain is to be on the constant lookout for solutions. One way we can start to do this is to ask ourselves the right questions, and not make definitive statements just because we don't currently know any other way to handle our situation. For instance, instead of automatically saying, "I've got this work that has to be done on this deadline; I cannot go outside right now and watch you play," instead ask, *How could I get my work done and also have my son be able to play outside?* When you start to ask yourself open-ended questions where you're expecting a great solution for everyone involved and not just making statements, you'll be surprised to find multiple solutions popping into your mind where you thought there were none.

Another way I started to train my brain is that I stopped making excuses for not having time to read. Reading is one of the ways you train your brain. Instead, I started to download audiobooks for free from the library and listen to them while I cleaned the house or drove to work. I'm discovering there's always a solution for what we're going through.

Hopefully by now you've gotten rid of the garbage, or at the very least, aren't consuming or creating it as often. Now you're holding on to what's helpful—in your ways of being, doing, and thinking. When you do that, you'll have positive outcomes, or at the very least, you'll be aware enough to change old patterns. Remember that the ultimate way to train your brain, besides trying to strong-arm it into submission, is to bathe it in the word of God. Until I bathed my brain in the word of God, I couldn't properly cleanse those lenses I saw through.

I found that reading scriptures helped me more than anything else. Advice from well-meaning friends doesn't always cut it, because they could just be trying to make you feel better, or they might be having a bad day themselves and unable to give you the best advice at the moment. God always tells the truth because He IS the truth. "...I am the way, the truth, and the life..." (John 14:6 NKJV). He says, "...we have the mind of Christ..." (1 Corinthians 2:16 NKJV). Think about that for a second. That verse is thrown around a lot, and I don't know if you've taken the time to consider what it means. Now let's talk about what the mind of Christ is and how it helps you.

Chapter Sixteen

Will You Become Part of His-Story?

When you have the mind of Christ, it means you're now able to understand things of a spiritual nature, discerning things in the spiritual realm. It's a higher understanding than we humans have in the natural realm, and beyond what an unbelieving person can understand or see. When you operate from this place, you understand the purpose and plan of God to restore humanity to its original splendor, and you see things from His perspective.

In the Old Testament, you find verses about how God wants to reveal things to you: "He reveals deep and hidden things; he knows what is in the darkness, and the light dwells with him" (Daniel 2:22 ESV). "He uncovers deep things out of darkness…" (Job 12:22 NKJV).

At that time, similar to how forgiveness had to be mediated through high priests, God usually only spoke to His prophets and select people. But when God showed up incarnate in the form of Jesus Christ, He became our Mediator and our Great High Priest. And before He ascended into Heaven, He said He was going to give us the Helper, aka the Holy Spirit. "But when the Helper comes, whom I will send to you from the Father, the Spirit of truth, who proceeds from the Father, he will bear witness about me" (John 15:26 ESV). He gave us the Holy Spirit to dwell in us.

The New Testament tells us that the mind of Christ is something every believer has access to. You don't have to go through a prophet or a holy man of God to get answers for what God wants you to know or to do. Jeremiah prophesied about this time that would come: "No more shall every man teach his neighbor, and every man his brother, saying, 'Know the LORD,' for they all shall know Me, from the least of them to the greatest of them, says the LORD" (Jeremiah 31:34, NKJV). You are living in those days now, where God speaks to you. God will download things to your mind you couldn't have known, and no human told you, but the Holy Spirit speaks to you. Here's how Paul describes it to the Corinthians:

"But we impart a secret and hidden wisdom of God, which God decreed before the ages for our glory. None of the rulers of this age understood this…." The smartest, most elite people of the day didn't understand it or grasp it. But "these things God has revealed to us through the Spirit." (That's the mind of Christ; that's the Spirit talking to you on a deeper level, beyond your human understanding and further than you can see in the natural state.) "For the Spirit searches everything, even the depths of God" (1 Cor. 2:7,8,10 ESV). If you asked Christ into your heart, you have the Holy Spirit, and if you're close to Him, He's constantly searching out the things of God to reveal to you and download in you, to give you an understanding no unbeliever could fathom.

"For who knows a person's thoughts except the spirit of that person, which is in him? So also no one comprehends the thoughts of God except the Spirit of God." "Now we have received not the spirit of the world, but the Spirit who is from God, that we might understand the things freely given us by God. And we impart this in words not taught by human wisdom but taught by the Spirit, interpreting spiritual truths to those who are spiritual. The natural person does not accept the things of the Spirit of God, for they are folly to him, and he is not able to understand them because they are spiritually discerned ... But we have the mind of Christ" (1 Corinthians 2:7-8,10-14,16 ESV).

To change what comes out, you must change what goes in

Now before you go on saying, "I've done too much wrong, I still sin every day. How could I have the mind of Christ?" I want to assure you that the mind of Christ is not just for perfect people, because only God is perfect. Even if others seem perfect or even tell you they are, that goes against God's word: "If we say that we have no sin, we deceive ourselves, and the truth is not in us" (1 John 1:8 KJV). You can have the mind of Christ and have the Holy Spirit living inside you and still be tempted, mess up, and fall sometimes. It's just like your home: You may have electricity connected to it, but if you don't flip on the light switch, you won't be able to see. Similarly, if you have the mind of Christ but choose not to use it, or you don't submit to the Holy Spirit living inside you, it's much harder to obey God or know the right thing to do. Yet now that you have the mind of Christ, it makes it easier for you to believe God when He tells you that you can do all things through Christ who strengthens you (Philippians 4:13).

It took me a while to believe all the good things God spoke about me and what I was capable of, because I hadn't been exposed to them enough. Remember, faith comes by hearing (Romans 10:17), and I wasn't hearing those scriptures every day. I was allowing myself to hear things the devil wanted me to hear instead. I was training my brain for pain, not gain. Once I started to listen to the audio Bible and sermons, and fill my mind with worship songs, I was able to accept God's word as truth. Is what you're listening to renewing your mind?

Here's how I started to change, though initially I didn't feel like I was smart enough and couldn't see myself the way God did. I still thought I was an idiot and a fool, that I was weak and not strong, but I found scriptures that helped me right where I was at, like, "...God has chosen the foolish things of the world to put to shame the wise, and God has chosen the weak things of the world to put to shame the things which are mighty" (1 Corinthians 1:27 NKJV). After reading His word, I knew that even in my broken and busted, weak and dumb (or so I thought) state, God could still use me for His purposes. And that gave me hope. It wasn't all over for me; good things could still be done in me and through me for the benefit of others and His kingdom. Knowing this made me happy and made me try harder and not give up or use my lack of intelligence on a certain topic as an excuse. If God can use the foolish, I figured I could be first in line.

If you're poor, you may think you're a nobody. Yet, "Has God not chosen the poor of this world to be rich in faith and heirs of the kingdom which He promised to those who love Him?" (James 2:5 NKJV). You may think, "I've done too many bad things," yet, if you ask God for forgiveness and you mean it, He promises, "He has removed our sins as far from us as the east is from the west" (Psalm 103:12 NLT). I promise you, whatever your excuse is for not loving yourself or not feeling worthy of the big, beautiful, awe-inspiring life God has for you, your excuse isn't valid. God has a plan specifically for you to accomplish and become something and someone so amazing, you won't recognize yourself. Believing God and taking the steps He needs you to will move you into that place.

You have everything already living inside you to become all you need to be to succeed in your calling. Sure, you may have to get some training and reprogram your mind. The truth is, all it takes is you believing in yourself and seeing yourself the proper way, admitting you've got a muddy way of looking at things. Take those lenses off to regain your sight!

God is able to use you in whatever state you are to bring Him glory and have you fulfill your purpose. When I realized that, it made me stop seeing myself as worthless and made me eager to begin self-study. I read more books and took more courses, confident now that God could use someone whom the world didn't see as smart and still make me successful. It motivated me to learn more and "Study to show thyself approved to God, a workman that needeth not to be ashamed" (2 Timothy 2:15 WEB). I didn't need to feel bad for where I was or what I didn't know. I needed to work hard and study to present myself properly, i.e., train my brain.

Of course, I no longer think I'm a fool, even though I thought I was for most of my life. But that's garbage I've gotten rid of. Now I hold on to what's helpful. And it's time for you to do the same, to believe the scriptures, including, "For with God nothing shall be impossible" (Luke 1:37 KJV). Imagine what would be possible for you and your life if you only took God at His word and believed you were worthy, and that His promises aren't just for others who seem to have their life more together, but they're for you too.

I've trained myself to trust in His word, even when it

seemed my brain had a difficult time remembering His word. There's even a scripture for that: "But the Helper, the Holy Spirit, whom the Father will send in My name, He will teach you all things, and bring to your remembrance all things that I said to you" (John 14:26 NKJV). The best teacher, trainer, and helper in the universe is the Holy Spirit, and He's here not only to teach us, but to remind us of everything the Father has told us. I got rid of the garbage. I stopped confessing I had a bad memory, or I wasn't smart, or any other insult or put-down I had for myself. This didn't happen overnight, because from a very young age, I started collecting insults, critiques, and criticisms, tucking them away in my mind to mull over later. After I got the revelation on how to regain my SIGHT rather than keep operating the way I had been, I held on to what was helpful by confessing God's word instead.

The best way to make history is to be part of His-story

Where are you right now? Are you seeing the challenges you're facing differently? Have you regained your sight, or are you still letting your real or perceived challenges stop you from doing great things? Are you feeling confident in who God created you to be, and going after your dreams? Have you been able to put into practice some of the things you've learned in this book, so that it's starting to make a difference?

As you may remember from Chapter Two, "God Created You on Purpose for a Purpose," there were some people in the Bible who may have seemed unlikely to amount to anything in life, whom God still used in powerful ways, and who made history. Here are a couple more I haven't mentioned. Gideon was hiding from the Midianites in a winepress when God called him to be brave and courageous and lead an army against those very enemies he was hiding from. There are people who had bad things happen to them, like Joseph, who was thrown into a pit because his brothers were jealous. He was sold into slavery and falsely accused of trying to rape someone, and ended up in prison.

Yet Gideon, even after God cut his army down from thousands to only 300, defeated his powerful enemies in a supernatural way. Joseph went from the pit to a prison and finally to a palace as God lined it up for him, even though he was a Jew, to become the second-most-powerful person in the land of Egypt, just under the king.

You can also find thousands more modern-day examples of people who, despite having big challenges to overcome, went on to make history. Beethoven became deaf, but he was still able to write such beautiful and transcendent music that a couple of hundred years later, we're still listening to it. Walt Disney was fired from his first job at the Kansas City Star after his newspaper editor told him he didn't have enough imagination or creativity. Yet he used his imagination to create Walt Disney Studios and theme parks, revolutionize animation, and win more Academy Awards than anyone else in history (22, plus four honorary ones, equaling 26 Oscars).

Oprah Winfrey was repeatedly molested by her cousin, uncle, and a family friend. She eventually ran away from home and, at age 14, gave birth to a baby boy who died shortly afterward. She didn't let her tragic past stop her. She was an honors student in high school, got a full scholarship to college, and now is worth $3 billion. Nelson Mandela was a lawyer and established Africa's first black law firm. He was working with the African National Congress (ANC) to end white minority rule and to stop racial segregation. The government banned the ANC, and Mandela and many other leaders were arrested for treason. Mandela was sentenced to life in prison and treated terribly while there. Yet when he got out of prison, he became the first black president of South Africa, and jointly won a Nobel Peace Prize for his efforts to end apartheid.

As with all these people, you too may have been through some difficulties or even horrific events that are unimaginable. Yet, despite what your life has been like up until now, God sees something in you that you may not even see in yourself. It's beyond your understanding, your traits, your skills, your talents, or what others think of you. It's beyond anything you can ask, think, or imagine, and it's according to His power that works in you (Ephesians 3:20). You don't have to be anything other than who you are. You, just the way you are, plus obedience to your great big God, make you absolutely worthy, loved, chosen, capable, unstoppable, and eventually victorious at anything you, together with God, attempt to do.

Now you're equipped and ready, because you've changed your perspective about yourself and your situation in a positive way. You're seeing yourself the way God sees you, as His favorite creation. You know God loves you and made you the way you are for a purpose. You don't have to change a thing about your outside, because you've now solved the inside problem. You can be confident in who you are, and there's no need to compare yourself to others. You now know where your true beauty comes from, and you can have good days no matter what you look like. You've developed your heart and soul to be strong and not cave in to the pressures of others, but stand firm in your convictions. You've made the separation between who you really are and the body you live in. You've learned to make the best of what you've got and not be desperate to change it.

You finally know once and for all that you are worthy, and you matter just as much as anyone else. Now you can live your life unashamed of who you are, how God made you, or what your talents and capabilities are. You're more confident and courageous to go after your dreams and make your mark in life.

I bet you're shining bright these days and people are noticing there's something different about you. But most importantly, you're noticing. You're bolder, you're standing up for what you believe in, you have made peace with the gorgeous creation you are, and you are going to go on and make a difference in your life and the lives of many others. Congrats for coming this far; you're a champion. I hope you finally believe how amazing you are.

Throughout this book, I've mentioned many examples of people with challenges who decided to overcome them and leave a legacy. I'm counting on the day when someone will be talking about you, singing your praises, talking about the things you did, and what you accomplished despite your difficulties. Now that you've removed your worldly lenses and have finally regained your SIGHT and have the mind of Christ, I'd like to know what people might write about you one day. What are you inspired to go out and do now that you know nothing is impossible for you? I can't wait to read what people will write about you. I can't wait to hear how you will make history. I can't wait to know how you'll be part of HIS-Story.

ONE LAST MESSAGE!

I hope that your way of seeing yourself has been totally transformed by reading this book, and that you now have the courage and confidence to go after all the dreams God has placed in your heart. You only get one chance in this life, so go after God with every breath you have and complete the work He gave you to do until the day He returns to get you.

Keep pressing forward. Always trust that God Who began a good work in you will complete it (Phil 1:6). Hold on to your hope and stoke the embers of faith in your heart, for there will be cold days ahead. God said that in this life we would have tribulation, but He also said, "…be of good cheer; I have overcome the world" (John 16:33 KJV).

Now that you know your worth and how much God loves you, you can go boldly into your future, because when you team up with God, you're unstoppable. People you don't even know yet are waiting for you to fulfill your dreams, because their lives will be changed by your faithfulness.

Whatever God gave you and however he made you, no one can belay you if God wants to display you

Acknowledgments

I would like to acknowledge people whose courage, perseverance, spirit of excellence, and example I've looked up to along my journey. You are those who've shined your lights so brightly, despite adversity, self-doubt, and the criticism of others. You've inspired dreams, and shown it was possible to be a success at living your purpose, while helping many along the way. I know because I'm one of them.

Joyce Meyer, it's beyond inspiring how you've not let your pain drown out your praise. Your matter-of-fact testimony of the God you serve makes all those who listen to you better. I often repost your messages on Instagram.

Angela Bassett, I've looked up to you since the 90s. Your style, grace, class, and how you handle adversity are worthy of emulation. You exude confidence. You're a beautiful balance of feminine beauty and strength. (And I'm not going to lie, I've envied your killer arm muscles!)

Dolly Parton, I don't even know where to begin. I feel your heart in your music. Your lyrics and voice make me cry (the good tears). Your relationship with the Lord is precious. Your witty one-liners (often at your own expense) I find myself quoting time and time again.

Viola Davis, your talent is a pinnacle I could only dream of reaching, and your acting is unparalleled. Thank you for fighting for your career despite every challenge and closed door. You've inspired hope in so many, and because of you, so many little girls know that not only are their dreams possible, but those dreams are worth fighting for.

Jennifer Garner, you exemplify a life well lived. The positivity, fun, and creativity you put out into the world make dark days lighter. Your contribution to humanity is seen, felt, and noticed. You've made more of a difference than you know.

Steve Harvey, you draw us in with your storytelling of where you've been and how you got there. You never stop sharing that your success is because of God. You're unapologetic about your faith. On breaks from filming when you could just go to your trailer or green room and relax, you sacrifice your personal time to share your faith and encourage others.

Dhar Mann, you gave me a safe space to practice my craft. You saw things in my acting range that others didn't, and you offered me roles that others wouldn't see me in. You've expanded me and my opportunities, and I'm grateful. You've shown grace and perseverance under pressure and opposition, and never returned evil for evil. Your passion and heart to do right have blessed many.

Trent Shelton, from the first time I heard you speak at a Brendon event many years ago, I was moved to tears. You ignited my secret dream of being a speaker, and it wasn't until I heard you that I felt there was a place for me, and that I could. Your heart, tenacity, and vulnerability made me believe that a rough-around-the-edges poet like me could also impact an audience.

Patricia Heaton, you're a tremendous example of someone who never gives up no matter how difficult the path. In an industry that doesn't always take kindly to those who are outspoken about their faith, your firm stance is stellar. Your comedy prowess cheers up a room and opens hearts.

Cheryl Salem, your connection with God makes me yearn to know Him more. When you speak, you challenge us to be better and get closer to Abba Daddy. You show us that anything is possible. You are so talented, and I've learned so much from your books and hearing you speak.

Myron Golden, your understanding of the scripture is so deep. I have lunch with you every day (watching your YouTube videos). The truth bombs you drop without worrying about ruffling feathers amaze me. Your business concepts should be studied in schools.

Mel Novak, you've taught me boldness like no other. Your heart to serve those in need is astounding (40 years of prison and homeless ministry). The way you pour your life into those who can't give back is inspiring. Your heart of love and hands of service remind me of Jesus.

Vince Galli, in a world of harshness, you've always been a gentle guide. Thank you for your patience, consistency, and giving me correction in a way that doesn't diminish me.

Garth & Virginia Hickey, your support and encouragement have always been a blessing. Thank you for being a sounding board and reading through the rough material and giving feedback when this book was only an idea.

ABOUT KATHERINE

Katherine is an encouragement coach and a loving caregiver, concerned about those people God has placed in her path. She desires to lead by example, showing you how to overcome your fears and realize how powerful you are so you can accomplish what you were put on this earth to do.

Katherine has written three previous books, all faith-based, self-help, quirky motivational "poetry with a punch" to help those mending from a broken past to strengthen their faith and gain the courage and confidence they need to go after their dreams.

She's also an actress in more than 100 projects for TV, film, theater, and commercials. She's a series regular on the wildly popular inspirational show on YouTube called *Dhar Mann.* Besides acting and authoring books, she's also a movie producer/director with multiple upcoming projects.

Katherine is the wife of her teenage sweetheart and a mom of two boys who are ten and a half years apart in age. Some have said she brings encouragement almost through osmosis to everyone she's around. She has an unshakeable optimism and loves to encourage others to trust God with all they've got.

ADDITIONAL RESOURCES

"THE DIVINE SOLUTION" ONLINE MINI-COURSE

Now that you've gone through the book, perhaps you've found yourself in the place I spoke about back at the end of Chapter 7, even if you didn't see it at the time. I've created this mini-course to help you finally get to the root cause of the overwhelm and pain in your life.

This is the solution you've been looking for to:

- heal your soul
- dry your tears
- decrease tension and anxiety

...and finally be able to breathe again.

The DIVINE Solution will help you find and fix whatever is causing you heartache related to your view of yourself, so you can leave your painful past behind, discover the right solution for you and live the rest of your life with joy and belief that the big, beautiful future you've only dreamed about is available to YOU!

This mini-course is *valued at $497,* but because you picked up this book, it's **yours for only $39.** Get "The DIVINE Solution" by going to KatherineNorland.com/Divine.

"YOU ARE WORTHY"
HOME STUDY ONLINE COURSE

Go deeper into gaining courage and confidence by finding out how to see yourself and love yourself the way God does, finally make peace with yourself, know you're enough, and have what it takes to reach your dreams. Found at KatherineNorland.com/Worthy

POETIC PRESCRIPTIONS FOR ETERNAL YOUTH

Shatter your misconceptions about image and self-worth in this truthful yet lighthearted look at our bodies, and the difference a divine perspective makes. Found at PoeticPrescriptions.com

POETIC PRESCRIPTIONS FOR PESKY PROBLEMS

With this scripture-based creative poetry, you will overcome doubt, grow your faith, and find freedom from your toxic thoughts. Found at PoeticPrescriptions.com

POETIC PRESCRIPTIONS FOR PLAGUING PROBLEMS

Life's issues can sometimes eat away at you, just like plagues right out of the Bible. They can stop you from living life to the fullest and may make you question where God is. This book will assist you in finally terminating those problems with God's help. Found at PoeticPrescriptions.com

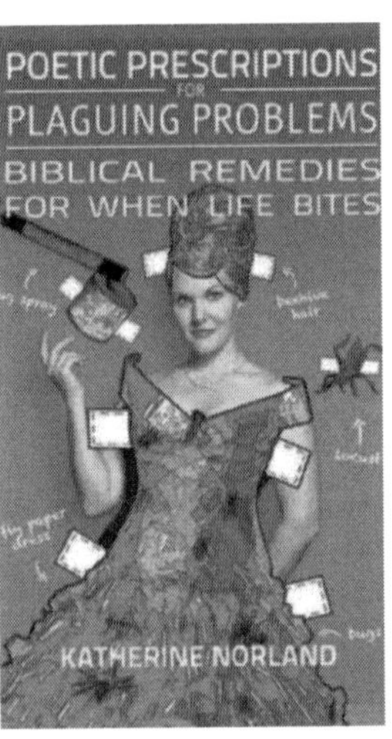

Special FREE Bonus Gift for You

To help you achieve more success, there are **FREE BONUS RESOURCES** for you at:

FreeGiftFromCoachKat.com

You'll get three in-depth training videos from my online course "You Are Worthy" to show you that no matter where you've been or what you've done, you can become an heir to God's promises and live an empowering, noteworthy life with joy and accomplishment!